WHA  YING...

"I am so happy that Richard's war story will be remembered in Victor's new book, *The Way It Was*. Richard was missing in action for two months and I am so thankful that he returned home. I think that his experiences made him the generous, kind, and loving person that he was."

—*Rose Heim, NY, NY*

"I am deeply grateful that I have had the opportunity to meet Mr. Morris Casey and hear his war experiences. I am anxiously awaiting the publication of Mr. Robilio's book, *The Way It Was*.

—*Marty H. Martin, Commander of the American Legion, Post 134, Horn Lake, MS*

"I am excited about Victor's new oral history book because I was part of the victory in World War II."

—*Lester Gingold, World War II Veteran, publisher of The Best Times*

"I am extremely proud of my husband, Sam Cox, for the brave service he gave for his country during World War II. My thoughts and prayers are always with his comrades who lost their lives in battle."

—*Audrey Cox, Memphis, TN*

"My fellow World War II Veterans from the 78th Lightning Division are looking forward to reading Victor's new book, *The Way It Was*, with great anticipation!"

—*Morris Casey, Technical Sergeant, 78th Lightning Division*

THE WAY IT WAS

DECEMBER 7, 1941 THROUGH AUGUST 15, 1945

You find in this book an "oral history" told to me personally from the World War II Veterans who were there. I have written down facts that were told to me verbally during the interviews. There may be some errors.

Censoring of World War II Veteran's letters was mandatory for security reasons. They are now speaking out about their World War II experiences. This book is uncensored and tells the truth about the way it was.

There will be mistakes in the oral history stories, but ninety eight percent of the facts are correct. Drop me a note if you find a mistake, and the second printing will be happily corrected.

The journals in the book that were written by the veterans are as is—with NO proofing. I cannot, nor will not, correct any grammar or syntax use by the veterans in their personal journals. The U.S. Air Force was called the army air corp during World War II. I have left it as Air Force throughout the book because most of the World War II veterans refer to it as that today.

—Victor L. Robilio, Jr.

WWII
THE WAY IT WAS

DECEMBER 7, 1941 THROUGH AUGUST 15, 1945

An oral history
by our brave and young
citizen soldiers.

7-23-11

VICTOR L. ROBILIO, JR.

Published by PREMIUM PRESS AMERICA

PREMIUM PRESS AMERICA gift books are available at special discounts for premiums, sales promotions, fund-raising, or educational use. For details contact the Publisher at P.O. Box 159015, Nashville, TN 37215, or phone toll free (800) 891-7323 or (615) 256-8484, or fax (615) 256-8624.

www.premiumpressamerica.com

Cover and interior layouts by Bob Bubnis/BookSetters

ISBN 9781933725086

Library of Congress Control Number 2007937396

First Edition January 2008
1 2 3 4 5 6 7 8 9 10

I would like to dedicate this book to:
My loving wife of 45 years, Kay Robilio; and
my two beautiful daughters, Catherine Robilio
Womack and Cecilia Robilio.

TABLE OF CONTENTS

ACKNOWLEDGEMENTS

1. Kay Robilio—Thanks to my wife for all of her encouragement and patience. Gratitude to her for understanding during the many hours that went into the writing of this book.

2. John R.S. Robilio—Thanks to my brother for his expertise relative to geographical and historical problems. He is fluent in the use of the German, Italian, and Spanish languages. John explained the many German phrases used by their Luftwaffe. He also helped with geographical areas of the Pacific Ocean.

3. "Chip" Womack—Thanks to my grandson for listening intensely to all of my WWII stories. He never got bored.

4. Norma Rogers—Thank you for all of your advice, enthusiasm, and encouragement.

5. Misty Moss—Thanks to my assistant and friend for all of her advice and help with getting this book on the word processor.

6. Pete Pinckney—Thanks to my college friend for his help in the use of naval verbiage about Pearl Harbor.

7. Many thanks goes out to the many living and deceased veterans who appeared on the Library Channel TV 18 Show, "Winds of History". I have interviewed over 200 Veterans over the past 30 years. They were the impetus for my oral history book.

8. Sincere gratitude to all of the families of the living and deceased veterans who have helped me with research and the use of their loved one's journals, letters, notes, and pictures.

9. Jeff Weintraub—Thank you for the use of your father's journals. You helped me stay on course. Jeff's father saved many civilian, Japanese, and American lives. The Japanese pictures, from his father's library, were beyond duplication.

10. Simon "Spider" Webb—Thank you for the use of your journals and also your two short stories, *The Parade* and *The Ranch*. Your openness and sense of humor gave me much enthusiasm. I also want to thank you for proofing the Marine and Naval terminology in many of the chapters. Your ideas about the layout of the book, the front (pictures of all four services) and back cover (especially your ideas of the flags and quotes from the great leaders of the free world). The before and after pictures helped gel my own thoughts about the World War II Veterans courage and tenacity.

11. Bob Shafer—Thank you for your encouragement and your keen sense of humor which helped keep me moving. Also, gratitude goes to you for proofing the terminology used in many of the Army and Army Air Corp chapters. Your devotion to America is remarkable and without duplication. You are indeed a very patriotic American.

12. Mary Battle—Gratitude to my University of Memphis English Professor between 1957 and 1961. Thank you for making me learn how to think and use my brain before I said anything verbally. Thank you for teaching me how to listen and not talk so much. I have admiration for you because of your devotion to the teaching profession. You taught me how to write.

13. John Harkins—Thank you for all of your help and research. I also want to thank you for all of your support over the years.

14. Ed Frank—Thank you for all of your research and support for the book.

15. Jim Johnson—Thank you for your support and finding some of the Veterans that I interviewed.

16. Andy Malone—Thank you for the use of your computer and help in scanning the pictures for this book.

17. Morris Casey—Thank you so much for the extra effort that you have put forth in helping with pictures for the book. Your help with the use of the 1944 and 1945 pictures, made by the signal corp of The 78th Lightning Division, is appreciated.

18. Paul and Shirley Vescovo—Many thanks to you for all of your help and encouragement.

19. Sam Cox—Much gratitude towards you for all of your help in the finding of pictures to help me complete this book. You and your wife, Audrey, have inspired me.

20. Crawford McDonald—Many thanks to you for all of you extra research on helping me with pictures and your insights on the book.

21. Herman "Red" Gonzalez and the book, *The Lightning: The History of the 78th Infantry Division*—Thank you so much for your help with picture usage of this book.

22. Last but certainly not least, thank you to my Mother and Father who encouraged me when I was young to appreciate and learn from history. They took my brother, John, and me to many battlefields, museums, historical buildings when we were growing up. My parents instilled a keen sense in my character that "history does repeat itself." They also taught me that liberty is kept alive only by our internal vigilance.

PREAMBLE

THIS BOOK IS A COMPILATION OF STORIES FROM THE many American Army, Navy, and Marine Corp Citizen patriots who fought for our great nation during WWII. Giant armies spawned by cruel dictators clashed with Democracy during this period of time. The unholy alliance between Communism and Democracy finally crushed the fascist leaders and totally destroyed their massive armies. Let us tumble back in history and learn about these American patriots.

This book is an "oral history" account of events that took place in WWII from copies of journals, old tapes and new DVD's that record each American Veteran's eyewitness account. I decided, in my book, "The Way It Was," that I use only factual information and recollections straight from the genuine battle weary Veterans who told the truth and didn't embellish each particular event.

American soldiers sometimes went for days without food. They also endured blistering heat in the South Pacific.

In Europe, the winter of 1944-1945 was one of the coldest ever for the combatants. The Battle of the Bulge actually went on for forty days and forty nights.

I, myself am a "Rock Patriotic," (as *described by Norma Rogers*), because I feel in my heart the emotions of the strong rock courage of our WWII Veterans. They made America what it is today. "Goose bumps" appear on my arms when I hear their stories. Iwo Jima oral history stories will often awake me from my peaceful sleep in the middle of the night. Without their unbelievable courage and grit we would be speaking German or Japanese. May God bless all of them!

NOTE: I have written this book from oral history interviews that I have had with the veterans. The journals that I have included in the making of this book were written by the World World II Soldiers themselves. I have not changed one single word from the journals. The way that they wrote it, is the way it was.

The Patrick Graney Family of Davenport Iowa: Sons and Daughters
—*Courtesy of Victor L. Robilio Jr.*

FORWARD

The U.S.A.
A Nation of Immigration

AFTER YEARS OF INTERVIEWING MANY GI's ON TV AND ALSO interviewing others personally, my opinions have crystallized. The total amount interviewed is about 200. 85% were World War II Veterans, and 15% were Korea and Vietnam Veterans.

Do we need Latino immigration? Yes, we need the immigrants. Why? We need them to revitalize our country's thoughts and energy. I am the grandson of an immigrant, John S. Robilio, from Northern Italy.

American sons and daughters of immigrants were very brave and performed heroic deeds during World War II. Some were fighting Japanese, Germans, Italians, Bulgarians, and Hungarians; while some were nurses and factory workers. All were protecting democracy and freedom.

Many American school children today have not been taught about the many sacrifices our U.S.A. families made during World War II. Some children think that America and Germany fought Russia during World War II.

Samuel Cox Jr. fought the Japanese in the mountains and jungles of New Guinea. His unit was outnumbered. They were starved "off and on" for months. Sam also suffered from 100 degree tropical rainforest temperatures. The humidity was also extremely high and uncomfortable. It rained everyday.

Sam's 200 man Guerilla unit was a sword in the side of a much larger Japanese force. His unit never gave up and it inflicted heavy casualties on the Japanese. He is a descendant of French Huguenot immigrants.

During World War II I had four uncles that actively served, as well as a black friend. Without these people and their sacrifices we would not be the country that we are today.

My uncle, Raymond Robilio, was stationed with the Army's Eighth Air Force in England. He was a sergeant. Uncle Raymond survived 25 missions as a Top Turret Gunner on a B17. He received the Distinguished Flying Cross Award. Uncle Raymond Robilio said one day, "The Sky was dark over England from B17s in the air heading towards Germany." He also said, "On Hitler's birthday each year the 8th Air Force always dropped a nice commode on Hitler's chancellery headquarters in Berlin."

Raymond Robilio, Sergeant, U.S. Army 8th Air Force
— *Courtesy of Michael Robilio*

My uncle, Eugene Robilio, was stationed in New Guinea with the United States Army. His unit was evacuated because of malaria and jungle diseases. My uncle, John S. Robilio Jr., was stationed in Washington D.C. with the Army. My other uncle, Silvio Robilio, was in the Army and was stationed in the Panama Canal area. George Bennett, my black friend, was wounded at Guadalcanal. He carried Japanese shrapnel near his stomach area all his life. My grandmother had four stars in the front window of her house, representing her four children serving in the two military services.

Sam A Sarno Sr. married my Aunt Louise, who was my Father's sister. He was a 1st Sergeant in a Military Police Company that was stationed at the Ferry Command in Memphis, TN. Their principal job, for the military, was security of the city of Memphis. Sam also transferred German and Italian POWs to a camp located at Como, MS.

Every Sunday at 1:00 pm, during World War II, we would all gather at Grandma Robilio's spacious home. Every one in the family, not on a tour of duty, would attend. As a five year old, I was overwhelmed by their patriotism and love for America!

Standing at Attention, Victor L. Robilio Jr., at age five. 1944 (Colonel Bushey behind him)

—*Courtesy of Victor L. Robilio Jr.*

Our Congress should vote for the visitor and work cards for the many skilled Latinos residing in our country. Congress should not let this problem fester. The elected members of Congress, who are not voting for a compromise on the immigration reform bill, are not leaders. They are much like the same narrow minded people who helped keep "Jim Crow" established during and after World War II.

Sam Sarno Sr. and Louise Robilio (on their wedding day)
—*Courtesy of Sam Sarno Jr.*

My "Grandma Robilio" relaxing on her porch in 1939.
—*Courtesy of Victor L. Robilio Jr.*

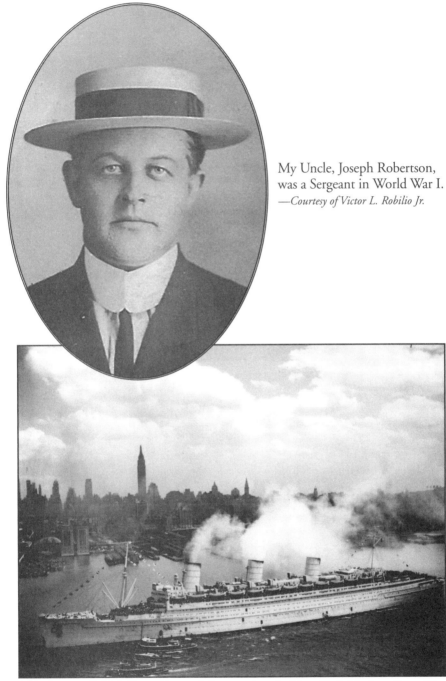

My Uncle, Joseph Robertson,
was a Sergeant in World War I.
—*Courtesy of Victor L. Robilio Jr.*

The famous British liner, Queen Mary, arrives in New York Harbor, June 20,
1945 with thousands of U.S. troops from European battles.

—*Courtesy of National Archives*

Line up of some women welders including the women's welding champion of
Ingalls. 1943
                                            —*Courtesy of National Archives*

HISTORICAL OVERVIEW

THE PRE-WORLD WAR II AMERICAN GENERATIONS WERE not pampered, spoiled, or bombarded by big government or televisions tasteless violence. Discipline, family character building, corporal punishment, and honesty were taught to them at home and at school.

Since World War II, big government entitlement programs have created "No Work Generations." Paying people that are unmarried to have children is counter productive! It is hard to find responsibility in a "No Work Generation." May God protect us from any US Congress that is causing "No Work Generations." The World War II generation is the one our Congress should always emulate. The God loving World War II generation needs to be our role model.

President Dwight D. Eisenhower is probably "rolling over" in his grave regarding our foreign policy mistakes. He often warned us about the dangers of the political, military, and industrial complex. Congressional apathy and questionable "think tanks" located in the U.S.A. have added to our foreign policy mistakes.

President George Washington warned us of the period of large standing armies.

President Teddy Roosevelt said, "Carry a big stick, but walk softly." This is the best policy! We need to love ourselves first and then love our country. Fellow inhabitants, adherence to, "Good world wide public relations prevents wars!"

My friend Joseph Post said, "The American family is still the backbone of America."

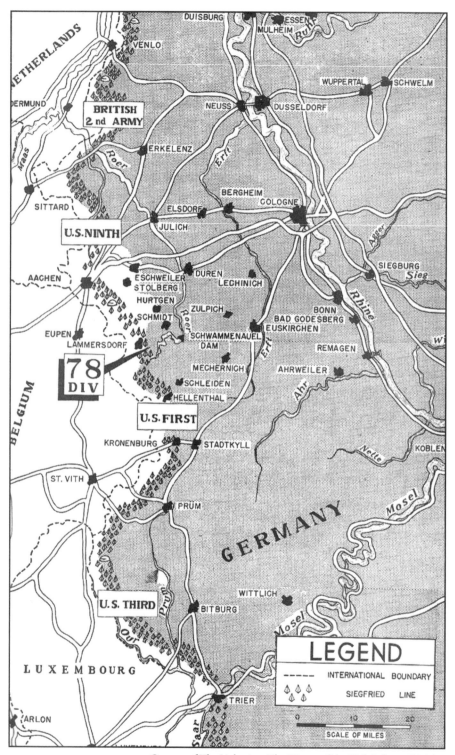

—*Courtesy of The Lightning: The History of the 78th Infantry Division*

MAPS:

THE GEOGRAPHY OF WORLD WAR II WAS NOT CLEAR TO THE Japanese or Americans. Many of the Japanese and American pilots simply got lost and their planes fell into the ocean when they ran out of fuel. Both sides were flying over thousands of miles of ocean with antiquated maps.

Admiral Chester W. Nimitz, Commander in chief of the Pacific Fleet, had a scary experience in 1942. His B-17 pilot got lost in trying to find Guadalcanal in the vast Pacific Ocean.

BGen Clements, FAdm Nimitz *, and Adm. Halsey at Yokosuka
—*Courtesy of National Archives'*

Fortunately, Nimitz's aid, Lt. Hal Lamar, had a 1942 National geographic Magazine in his briefcase. It had a map of the large area inside of it that they happened to be flying over. They used this map to locate successfully Guadalcanal. They had been flying over a Japanese held island that was not on the old Army Air Corp map, but was on the new National Geographic map. If Lt. Hal Lamar had not tossed the map in his briefcase at the last minute, to look at it on the trip, well…. you write the story.

Army Air Force G2, Sam Weintraub, while on the Ellise Islands at a U.S. Airfield experienced great frustration with eighteen lost Corsairs. Sam was on duty during a bad storm when eighteen Corsairs were doing a bomb run from Tarawa and got lost in the storm. He picked them up on radar and communicated with them by voice, but they had poor maps and horrendous storms flailed them; therefore, they should have never been sent out. They all ran out of gas and had to crash land near various islands. The PBY's and a destroyer picked up at least fourteen or fifteen of them, but they were still one hundred miles off from his Ellice Islands. This information emanated from Sam Weintraub's personal journal.

CHAPTER I
THE BATTLE FOR NEW GUINEA
Story of Samuel Cox Jr.

SAMUEL COX WAS WONDERING HOW HE GOT TRAPPED FOR nine days behind Japanese lines with his guerrilla group. As the Japanese sprayed the fox holes, from two directions, his wounded buddies screamed in pain for his help. He then recalled that General McArthur was an "egocentric maniac" and would not pull out his unit, even against the Army doctor's "stiff request" for rest and relaxation. The men looked like Christ taken down from the cross.

Samuel Cox Jr
—Courtesy of Sam Cox. Jr.

Sam recalled the whole New Guinea campaign while he was sleepless at night, trapped in his foxhole. Part of his division was sent to the Coast on the Northeastern part of the Owen Stanley Mountains to open up a second front. Sam's 200 man patrol was trained in Commando tactics, hand to hand combat, use of the knife, and the use of a wire on the Japanese necks for a silent kill. They were sent directly from the South over the Owen Stanley Mountains.

Sam's grandfather had a rice plantation on the banks of the Mississippi River. It was some 30 miles upstream from New Orleans. The population of the community consisted mostly of people of Cajun descent. Sam's family is not Cajun as his ancestors originated from England and France.

During the depression, Sam spent more than nine years as a youth on the plantation with his grandparents and was exposed to the Cajun way of life. Often times, he spent weekends with Cajun trappers in the swamps. This exposure gave him valuable experience and knowledge of how to read the trees for direction, manage insect bites, swamp heat, gators, snakes, and survival under adverse conditions. This experience allowed him to survive in the jungles of New Guinea. His unit was down to 18 men left of the original 200 guerrillas when they came out of entrapment and the jungles.

He recalled in foxhole dreams about how the Aussie railroad system was not standardized. They had to load and unload three times to move his own division. The Aussies expected an invasion, should they lose New Guinea to the Japanese.

Crossing the Equator on their way to Australia. The ship they traveled on was the U.S.S. Lauriline.

—Courtesy of Sam Cox Jr.

Crossing the Equator—This involved their head being shaved and being paddled. Before they cross the equator they are considered a pollywag, after crossing they become a shellback. They were initiated by King Neptune and his court.

—Courtesy of Sam Cox Jr.

Sam left Brisbane, Australia for the trip to Port Moresby, New Guinea. It was very difficult to say the least. The Coral Sea was terribly rough as waves broke over the deck of the Liberty ship. It was loaded with 55 gallon drums of aviation fuel. Next loaded was 500 pounds of bombs. Then a hatch cover was placed over that. Troops were then loaded in the hatch hole below deck. We slept on cold steel with a loaded pack as a pillow. A wooden ladder was constructed so we would climb to the deck to use the restroom, which was a challenge in the darkness. Japanese submarines were very active around us.

When we disembarked from the ship at night in the Port Moresby harbor we had to climb down rope ladders and be tendered ashore. All port facilities were bombed out. It was literally covered with sunken Allied ships. The Japanese were just 25 miles outside of the city limits.

New Guinea is shaped like a big rooster. The left side belonged to the Dutch, and the right side belonged to the Aussies. It was a tropical rain forest. It was the monsoon season and it rained eight inches every day.

"Our first encounter with Japanese was when I saw them coming down a path, led by a bespeckled Japanese Lieutenant. They were in single file. Our unit of 12 men simply moved into the tall Kuni grass to the right of the trail. When their last man passed our first man, we opened fire. We dropped about 30 of them and disappeared back into the heavy jungle and headed back to our base camp."

Alone with a native guide, I had my second encounter with the Japanese. We came across a deserted village that had been looted by "Empire of the Sun" soldiers, and had been partially burned. Three things were very sacred to all natives of New Guinea: First are their pig, then their garden, and finally their wife. This village had no women, gardens, or pigs. The Japanese had abused and/ or used all three. After this encounter, I was treated to some food and drink by a few of the natives, when all of a sudden I was told by my guide that three Japanese were approaching us. I hid in an empty grass hut and waited for all three to get close to me. I threw a hand grenade between them and it instantly dropped all of them permanently.

My only encounter with "Head Hunters" was high up in the Owen Stanley Mountains. We walked thru their village observing Japanese shrunken heads on tall poles outside of the main gate. They hated the

Japanese with a passion for their abuses. One head hunter looked at my red hair and full red beard, and then he ran this tongue around his mouth. I immediately patted my M-1 rifle and said, "No touche, big stick bites."

Food and ammunition was our biggest problem. We depended on an air drop every 3rd day. Often times the monsoon rain created fog in the mountains and we couldn't have a drop. There were times we went 3 to 6 days without a drop and had to live off the land grubs and lizards which were in abundance. The planes tried to weigh down our parachuted supplies, so that they would penetrate the rain forest. The forest had very thick tree top foliage. One or two planes crashed trying to get supplies to us, when we were in very tight positions. At intermittent times we starved.

(Above) All of the Medals that were achieved by Sam Cox (Opposite) Sam Cox and a Kangaroo that he befriended in Australia.

—*Courtesy of Sam Cox Jr.*

In the later part of November 1944, what was left of our rag-tag division led a drive on Sananawda to cut the Japanese into two pockets. We had their back bottled up against the

South Pacific. On December 14, 1942 I took a mortar shell to the lower spine. Seven days later we were rescued in the middle of the night by one of our patrols. I entered New Guinea weighing 187 lbs. At the end of the 9 ½ months of combat and when hospitalized, I weighed 110 lbs.

YOU HAVE TO BELIEVE

You have to believe in happiness,
Or happiness never comes.
I know that a bird chirps none the less
When all that he finds is crumbs.
You have to believe the buds will blow—
Believe in the grass in the days of snow;
Ah, that's the reason a bird can sing,
On his darkest day he believes in Spring.
You have to believe in happiness—
It isn't an outward thing.
The Spring never makes the song, I guess,
As much as the song the Spring.
Aye, many a heart could find content,
If it saw the joy on the road it went,
The joy ahead when it had to grieve,
For the joy is there—but you have to believe.
—Douglas Malloch.

Poem that was sent to Sam by his wife during World War II.
—*Courtesy of Sam Cox Jr.*

Audrey and Sam Cox
—*Courtesy of The Commercial Appeal, Memphis, TN*

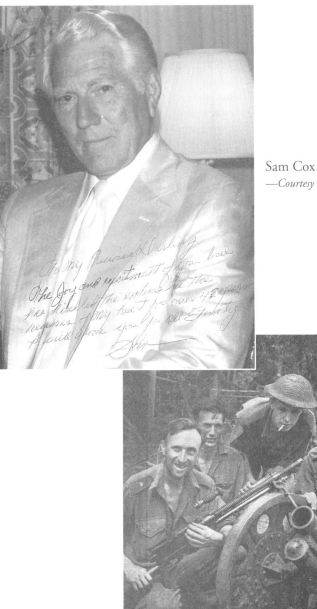

Sam Cox
—*Courtesy of Sam Cox Jr.*

Some Australian men and a captured Japanese canon.
—*Courtesy of Sam Cox*

Mike Burbage (in the center)

—Courtesy of Joan Burbage Hawkins

CHAPTER II
PEARL HARBOR ATTACK EYEWITNESS

Story of Mike Burbage

THE DATE IS SUNDAY, DEC. 7, 1941. MIKE BURBAGE IS THE officer of the day aboard the USS Detroit, a light cruiser. As a recent Annapolis graduate, he was wearing his dress white uniform. Most of the Pacific fleet USA sailors are heading for 7am church services aboard their ships. Mike's ship is anchored on the other side of Ford Island, across the island from Battleship row at Pearl Harbor.

It is a beautiful Sunday morning at Honolulu on the Hawaiian island of Oahu. Many golfers and tennis players are out enjoying the weather. Everyone else on the island is trying to wake up in order to attend services or they are resting after a festive Saturday night.

Mike has the job of getting the USS Detroit ready for Sunday morning inspection. During inspection, all the pacific fleet's water tight compartments are open and their anti-aircraft guns are without shells. This was normal procedure for the Navy on inspection day.

Japanese Vice Admiral, Chuichi Nagumo, in the early a.m. released 186 planes: fighter planes, torpedo planes, dive bombers, and high altitude horizontal bombers at the U.S. Fleet anchored inside Pearl Harbor. This was his first wave of attack planes. He was to launch 176 planes in a second wave about an hour later. The second wave consisted of high altitude horizontal bombers, fighter planes and dive bombers. No torpedo planes were included in this second wave of attack planes. A third wave was to be sent, but it was called off by Nagumo for fear of the American Aircraft Carriers and their returning retaliation.

Commander Mitsuo Fuchida led the raid. He used "radio station finding equipment" tuned to radio station Honolulu to stay on the course for Pearl Harbor. The U.S. Army had a radar station operating on the north side of Oahu. It actually picked up the Japanese first wave. They were about one-hundred and thirty two miles from Pearl Harbor. The army duty officer at Fort Shafters thought they were the B17 army bombers coming from San Francisco and didn't alert anyone.

On his entering Pearl Harbor, he was to send up one flare to signal the torpedo planes to attack. The torpedo planes missed seeing his signal. He then sent up two flares so the dive bombers would attack. Those two flares did initiate the dive bomber attack.

A little later, three waves of torpedo planes attacked the American Naval Battleships: California, West Virginia, Nevada, Arizona, Maryland, Tennessee, Pennsylvania and Oklahoma. One large Japanese submarine and five midget submarines were sunk during the day. Another large Japanese submarine got away after firing on one of our cruisers that was leaving the harbor, fortunately it missed our ship.

Mike Burbage was viewing the Japanese planes attacking Battleship Row. They looked like a swarm of angry red wasps. Suddenly, a torpedo plane whizzed by in front of Mike, at deck level, it was so close he could see the Japanese pilot. Mike ran for the locked up anti-aircraft magazine shell storage room and quickly passed out the needed ammunition boxes. After pounding Battleship row with torpedoes and bombs, the Japanese planes turned toward the USS Detroit and her sister ship, The USS Raleigh, a light cruiser. Luckily the USS Detroit was missed by a Japanese torpedo, that went under its stern. The unexploded torpedo was recovered later. They also dropped 550 lb. bombs at the USS Detroit and her sister ship. The bombs missed but went very deep into the harbor mud. Mike was covered with mud from head to toe. He thanked God for the mud! The light cruiser, the Raleigh, was hit by a torpedo and sank immediately. Three Japanese

—Courtesy of Joan Burbage Hawkins

dive bombers dropped 550lb bombs at the Detroit, but missed during the second wave attack.

The captain of the Detroit, realizing the Japanese's goals, upped anchor as the second attack subsided. He knew a third attack would probably be in the works. The USS Detroit was guided carefully and slipped out of Pearl Harbor to look for Japanese aircraft carriers.

At Hickam Field, a Navy Priest was getting his altar set for Sunday Mass. Suddenly a Japanese dive bomber's load hit the mess hall. 35 died instantly and many more were wounded. He ran to a nearby machine gun emplacement, carried the gun to his altar, and mounted it. He let loose a wall of bullets at the many Japanese planes buzzing around Hickam Field. A song was written later that he inspired; it was called "Praise The Lord and Pass The Ammunition".

Twelve Army Air Corp B17's from San Francisco, low on fuel, tried to land at Hickam Field during the first attack. One was destroyed, but eleven made it to a safe place on the island. One actually landed on a golf course!

The Japanese planes overlooked a fuel ship, The USS Neosho, containing over 3 million gallons of aviation fuel. Its destruction could

Mike Bourbage-Flight Training on Vero Beach, FL,1943 (top row, 3rd from left)
—*Courtesy of Joan Burbage Hawkisns*

have been catastrophic for our Pacific fleet. They also missed millions of gallons of oil storage in underground tanks. Vice Admiral Nagumo wanted to destroy the fleet only, not the facilities. Fortunately, our aircraft carriers were at sea, or they too would have been sunk or damaged.

Mike Burbage told me that the American Fleet actually shot down 29 Japanese planes on that day of infamy. The Japanese Aircraft Carriers also had to dump another 32 planes at sea that were badly damaged.

The USS Enterprise ESSEX Class Air Craft Carrier sent planes to land at Pearl Harbor during the night of December 7th. They were mistakenly shot at by friendly fire. The USS Arizona still sits on the floor of Pearl Harbor with the memorial platform on top of her. A Japanese bomb hit her magazine. Around 1,000 naval personnel were killed when she exploded.

Mike Burbage went on to become a Navy fighter pilot. He was aboard the USS Franklin, an ESSEX Class Carrier at the battle of Okinawa. A Japanese plane dropped two 550lb bombs that severely damaged the Franklin during the battle. 500 were killed and 1,500 were wounded aboard the Franklin.

Captain Charles Lee "Mike" Burbage was born on February 28, 1918 and died October 15, 2006. His spirit will always be with us; his courage should be emulated by future generations of Americans.

Mike and Mary Bourbage on their Wedding day. 1942
—*Courtesy of Joan Burbage Hawkins*

Mike Bourbage
—*Courtesy of Joan Burbage Hawkins*

Morris Casey

My old Buddy

CHAPTER III
MORRIS CASEY AT THE REMAGEN BRIDGEHEAD & THE RUHR RIVER DAMS

Story of Morris Casey

MORRIS CASEY, MY FRIEND FROM WALLS, MISSISSIPPI HAD been to "German hell" and back. He was saved from death by wearing his steel helmet at the Remagen Bridgehead. He was a forward artillery sergeant, out in front of the American line, and in harms way.

Morris grew up in Whitehaven, Tennessee, a suburb of Memphis at that time. He did his basic training at Fort Oglethorpe, Georgia. His expertise was in the U.S. 105 Howitzer artillery weapon, a German tank destroyer. He was assigned to the 78th Infantry Division (Lightning Division) of the 3rd Battalion, 310th Infantry Regiment, rotating between the 1st and 9th Armies. Morris was involved in both the capture of the Ruhr River Dams and the seizure of the Ludendorff Railroad Bridge at Remagen, Germany. He helped train thousands of U.S. Army troops until he was needed in Europe in the fall of 1944.

Morris and Sarah Casey
—Courtesy of Morris Casey

His army unit was transported by ship convoy to Plymouth, England. The Lighting Division then embarked for LaHarve, France in October of 1944. On December 13, 1944, the "Battle

43

of the Bulge" began. Morris was a close witness to the capture and/or death of the "Green" Troops of the 106th and 28th Divisions of the U.S. Army. The Battle of the Bulge went on for forty days and forty nights.

Battle of the Bulge- 78th Lightning Division (Fighting for Survival from starvation, while the Germans watched. Yes, they did catch the cow to ward off starvation)

—Courtesy of Morris Casey

Battle of the Bulge- 78th Lightning Division

—Courtesy of Morris Casey

After the Battle of the Bulge, Patton's 3rd Army and the rest of the Allies had killed over 125,000 Germans and had only 80,000 dead and wounded. The very, very cold weather had added casualties on both sides, Allied and German.

Morris Casey witnessed Buzz Bombs (V I's and V II's) in the air heading for England and Antwerp. He saw action on the Siegfried Line with its "Dragons Teeth" Tank Stoppers. He was also involved in the Hurtgen Forest Battles.

He viewed two American Army Divisions decimated in front of the Ruhr River Dams. At the town of Schmidt, the retreating and badly mangled German Army left tank mines buried along with antipersonnel booby traps on all roads. At the Ruhr River Dams, Morris viewed the inside of a concrete German bunker with a dead German soldier in the rigor mortis position, still sitting up with a bullet thru his forehead. Morris lost a friendly Rifle Company Captain and his personal driver outside the bunker, when their Jeep drove over a land mine. The Jeep, driver and the Captain were catapulted into the air by the enormous blast.

A demolished bridge over one of the smaller Ruhr River dams.
—*Courtesy of Lightning: The History of the 78th Infantry Division*

Morris' boss, Lieutenant Colonel Harry Lutz used a ½ track and really worked the Germans over. He slipped thru their various traps on more than one occasion. He was a tall, resonant, resolved, and a strong willed Jewish officer who was not scared of the devil himself, let alone any German troops. All of the soldiers of the 310th Infantry Regiment loved him. Lt. Colonel Harry Lutz, 3rd Battalion Commander (Dec. 13, 1944 until March 14, 1945) received the Legion of Merit and the Silver Star and a Purple Heart for his bravery and leadership while in active combat against the German Army.

Lieutenant Colonel Lutz asked Technical Sergeant Morris Casey to bring forward three 105 Howitzers and their crews to start the Remagen Bridge Attack. Captains and Lieutenants were passed over because Technical Sergeant Casey was the best-trained expert on the 105 Howitzer, in the 78th Lightning Division.

—*Courtesy of The Lightning: The History of the 78th Infantry Division*

Remagen Bridge
—*Courtesy of The Lightning: The History of the 78th Infantry Division*

Remagen Bridge
—*Courtesy of The Lightning: The History of the 78th Infantry Division*

The railroad bridge at Remagen was still up when Morris arrived. All the other bridges that crossed over the Rhine were blown up by the retreating German Army. "Ike" could not believe it. It saved thousands of Allied lives. The 310th Infantry Regiment, 78th Lightning Division of the 1st Army and the 9th armor division worked with the tanks and 105 Howitzers, and captured the Remagen Bridge on March 7, 1945, at 3:50 p.m. Then the 1st Army and Armor Division 9th tanks, troops, and supplies poured over it for ten days and ten nights until it fell in to the river.

Morris was wounded on the high ground one evening, across the Rhine from Remagen, when an artillery shell hit a tree above his foxhole. He had his helmet on, but received nine pieces of shrapnel in his body. He was transported across the river by boat the next day. The bridge was a one-way avenue for the Allies into the heart of Germany. He returned to the 78th Lightning Division after a two-month hospital stay in both Belgium and France. The Division went all the way to the Elbe River. On their way they captured 900 cities, took 300,000 prisoners, and suffered 1,500 dead.

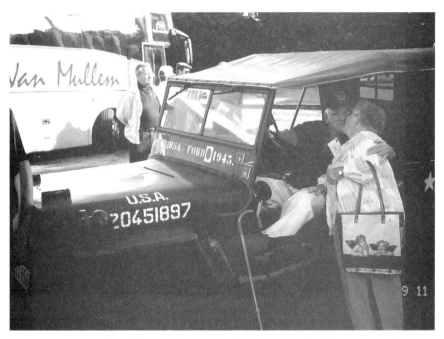

Morris and Sarah Casey- Visiting Germany and Belgium (2004)
—Courtesy of Morris Casey

David Noel Thompson
—*Courtesy of David Noel Thompson Jr.*

CHAPTER IV
THE ROYAL CANADIAN AIR FORCE
GUNNER &
THE FRENCH UNDERGROUND

Story of David Noel Thompson

DAVID THOMPSON WAS SHOT DOWN IN OCCUPIED FRANCE. He lived there for four months. David had help from the brave French underground and this is his personal story of bravery.

David was from near Newcastle in Northumberland, England. At age 16, in 1940, his father sent him from Blitz ravaged England to work for Nickey Brothers Lumber in Memphis, TN. He was to learn the lumber business as an apprentice. David had promised the British authorities, when he became of age, that he would help his country. He promptly joined the Canadian RAF as a gunner in 1942. He was trained at Quebec and other Canadian RAF bases.

David was sent to England and assigned to RAF 405 Squadron which was a pathfinder group. They would mark the targets for RAF night bombing raids against Berlin and other important targets. David was the top turret gunner and he would search the night sky for approaching German fighters.

From August 31, 1943 until January 2, 1944 David had made a total of 18 missions. His British bomber, Lancaster, had a crew of seven people. On their way back from Berlin, near Calais, France, David said probably a German night fighter slipped unnoticed under two of his squadrons' planes and fired a perpendicular machine gun through their underbelly. The Lancaster had no bottom ball turret gunner like our American B17 plane. No one could see the black painted German Fighter. As the burst of bullets tore through, David heard a painful scream on the intercom. He immediately grabbed his parachute and bailed out. The engineer also got out but the other five went down with the plane. David pulled the rip cord and passed out until he hit about 1,000 feet and then was fully conscious again.

David was fortunately picked up shortly after landing on the French soil by Rene' Guittard and Mary Terese of the French underground. He stayed at their home.

The Germans reported to the Red Cross at the plane's crash site the following information: (3) bodies were un-identified; (2) bodies were identified; (1) Engineer was captured and (1) was reported missing. The Red Cross told the Canadian families, but until David was captured, the four Canadian families didn't know who of the one missing and the three unidentified was actually alive. David was not captured for four more months while he lived with the French underground.

David lived with Madame Coquide and her niece Louise in the countryside for a while. He was then sent onto Paris where he and an American B26 Pilot Richard Miller stayed with Madame Fernandez in her Paris apartment. They were safe for a while but one day the Gestapo murdered Madame Fernandez's a friend who was a member of the same French Paris underground cell. She came in very excited and said, "Get out before the Gestapo finds you!"

Madame Fernandez hurriedly sent David Thompson and Richard Miller to Toulouse on a 10 hour train ride. In Toulouse he was told to ride a bike to the large city park and meet a man in a "blue suit" on a bench near the entrance. David was the *only* flyer of the seven assembled that could speak French and the blue suited man was to lead all seven of them out of France into neutral Spain.

As earlier agreed upon, they boarded a slow French train for Spain. All seven flyers would have to follow the Frenchman in the blue suit with *no speaking* while walking single file. The train stopped about a half mile from the Spanish border. Then, the seven flyers, in single file, followed the resistance man in the blue suit. He made a horseshoe path as the train pulled out. As they crossed the train tracks, something went wrong as three German border guards appeared and stopped all eight of them for questioning. David was second to be interrogated. They let the blue suit man go since his papers were in order. David could speak French and told them that he was a French Secretary. They asked him the name of the machine that he used to type letters on and he suddenly couldn't remember what a typewriter was called in French. They found him out!

David had stitched his RAF dog tags in his belt. When he showed it to them, they stripped him and beat him black and blue. Afterwards, a very obese French Vichy officer came in and put a pistol to his right temple. He demanded to know what was going on and who the other six flyers were. David shut up and he wouldn't tell him a "damn thing".

They put David and Richard Miller in a straw-bedded jail cell for a few days. The lice in that jail were so bad that Richard and David took turns picking lice from the hair on each others heads to pass the time. After that he and Richard were sent on a long train ride to Luft I, located near Gdansk, Poland. It was also near the cold Baltic Sea. Their meals consisted of brown bread with sawdust inside, brown water and watery potato soup. The New Zealand POWs knew how to make anything from tin cans so that they all could cook regularly. The welded tin cans served as their actual heated oven. Red Cross packs were given to them by the German guards regularly. They got 17 packs for 21 flyers so they had to share it all. David couldn't get the cakes that they had cooked to rise so they added forty Vitamin C Tablets from the Red Cross pack to the mixture. To their dismay, this was to no advantage. Nothing would get those cakes to rise. "D Bars" or candy bars became their barter tool.

Around May 3, 1945 the German guards departed. On May 5th a Russian Scout arrived at Luft I and said they were free. He said that Russian Armies were on their way to capture Berlin. On May 12, 1945, a stream of American B17's landed at Ravensbrook Air Dome near Gdansk and flew 7,500 allied airmen to Southern England to be rehabilitated.

David Thompson passed away in 2006 and we will always cherish his story of his courage and tenacity. He reminded us of all the allied soldiers' struggles and bravery during WWII.

Jubilant American soldier hugs motherly English woman and victory smiles light the faces of happy service men and civilians at Piccadilly Circus, London, celebrating Germany's unconditional surrender. May 7, 1945

—Courtesy of National Archives

David Noel Thompson
—Courtesy of David Noel Thompson Jr.

Bob Watson

—Courtesy of Murfy Nix

CHAPTER V
THE SEAHORSE ARMY ENGINEER
Story of Reverend Bob Watson

ON THE NIGHT OF JANUARY 12, 1945, A SINGLE JAPANESE plane dropped a bomb that landed beside Bob Watson's foxhole. Fortunately, it didn't explode. Bob just knew it was a dud! He immediately thanked God for saving his life.

The 534th Engineer Battalion members were trying to set up what the 6th Army of McArthur needed. They were trying to finish off the Japanese in the Philippines. The Chief Actor was General Douglas MacArthur. The U.S. Army units were in the process of crushing the Imperial Japanese Army. The city of Manila and the Philippine Islands were being liberated after three years of harsh Japanese occupation. Bob's engineer battalion had moved huge quantities of aviation fuel from Buna, New Guinea to the Leyte Gulf. The Army Air Force was thirsty for fuel .

A huge Japanese 240mm railroad cannon lobbed shells at Bob's 534th U.S. Army engineer battalion. The date was January 11, 1945. They were working on the beach in the Philippines at Lingay Gulf. The Japanese had brought the cannon over from Corregidor. It was American made and had been confiscated by the Japanese in 1942.

A shell landed on top of a U.S. Army ammunition truck near Bob's foxhole and exploded like a centennial fireworks exhibition. Eventually the 37th U.S. Army Infantry attacked and shut down the big cannon.

Bob's mind tumbled back to how he got in this situation. As a member of the U.S. 6th Army, he was brought to the western end of New Guinea first. Geographically, New Guinea looks like a "prehistoric bird" set on the top of a near circular Australia. The head was called the *Vogelkop*. It is the world's second largest island next to Greenland.

Bob enlisted when he was just 18 years old. He trained in Florida at camp Gordon Johnston in November, 1943. It was nothing like Buna, New Guinea.

The Western end of New Guinea was the most inhospitable place in the world for fighting a war. Many of the engineers suffered from: denge fever, malaria, typhus, dysentery, insects, snakes, crocodiles, and a multitude of Japanese snipers high up in the trees. Three missing engineers were probably eaten by crocodiles while they were swimming.

Everywhere that the Japanese landed troops, the local Native people were abused. They created forced labor and terrible treatment. The Japanese devoured their gardens. They killed their pigs; and physically and sexually abused the Native women.

McArthur used island hopping and bypassing of entire Japanese armies as his victory plan. Bob's unit traveled from Buna and the Vogelkop to the island of Morotai. It was northeast and toward the Philippines. Three airfields were built on Morotai to pound the Japanese in the Philippines. Rabaul and Truk islands were leap frogged. Wewak and Sarmi, in western New Guinea, were also bypassed. The Japanese 18th Army was dug in at Wewak. Rubaul island had over 100,000 Japanese troops there. It was heavily fortified and their main Japanese supply base.

The book *Seahorse Soldiering* by Robert Meredith Watson, Jr. is one of the best accounts I have ever read about MacArthur's Amphibian Engineers and the Battles of New Guinea and the Islands between New Guinea and the Philippines.

Bob Watson and I have been friends for over thirty years. He was truly a historian's historian. He was an Ordained Episcopal Minister and a close personal friend of mine and my wife, Judge Kay Robilio. Bob left a lasting impression on the development of my character. He was a very brave man who left me with much to think about in terms of bettering my family and my life. May his spirit always be with America and all of the Americans.

Bob Watson (Top Row, Far left)
—*Courtesy of Murfy Nix*

Bob Watson
—*Courtesy of Murfy Nix*

JM Taylor (far right)

—Courtesy of JM Taylor

CHAPTER VI
THE FLYING TIGER

Story of JM Taylor

J. M. TAYLOR HAD THE MOST UNUSUAL EXPERIENCES OF any officer that I have ever interviewed on TV. "JM's home is in Grand Junction, TN (not too far from Memphis) but he was living and working in Memphis when it all began. This is his story, the way he remembers it.

On December 7, 1941, America was pulled into the war by the Japanese sneak attack on Pearl Harbor and our other Pacific Military Bases. A few months later "JM" wanted to enlist but his parents refused to sign the required permit for one under twenty-one years of age. He was nineteen. At his defense job his co-workers were discussing going into the U. S. Army Aviation Cadet program and he was fixated toward that end. When he turned twenty and received his "Greetings" from Uncle Sam he convinced his parents to agree for him to apply for the Cadet program. He was accepted on September 16, 1942.

JM was successful in completing the pilot training program and eventually was sent to China in the summer of 1944 as a replacement pilot in the Fourteenth Air Force "Flying Tigers", General Claire Lee Chennault, commander. JM was fortunate to be assigned to the 75th "Flying Tiger Sharks" of the Twenty-third Fighter Group. His squadron's first Commander (Shark One) was the famed "Tex" Hill. Tex had been a squadron leader in the AVG and later was the group commander. The American Volunteer Group (AVG) were mercenaries released from the US military and were called The Flying Tigers by the Chinese and the name stuck and is still in use by their descendants.

The AVG entered combat late in December 1941 and were "slugging it out" with the Japanese until they were disbanded on July 4, 1942. Some of the men remained and were given rank in the US Army Air Force. The AVG was replaced by the Twenty-third Fighter Group: seventy-fourth, seventy-fifth and seventy-sixth fighter squadrons. All supplies had to be flown over "The Hump" (the treacherous Himalayan Mountains) as all ports with access to China and Burma were held by the "Empire of the Rising Sun". Only Indian ports were held by the Allies. This continued until the war's end.

JM flew P-40s early on and then the newer P-51s in 1944. "Blood Chits" or Nationalist Chinese Identification was issued to all flying personnel. Should any be downed local Chinese, civilian and/or military would render all aid possible getting them back to an Allied base because of the "Blood Chit". It was written in Chinese characters and said that "all people military and civilians should give all aid to the foreigner who has come to defeat the enemy", roughly translated. The returned flyers rejoined their squadrons and returned to combat, some more than once.

On November 11, 1944 (the old WW I Armistice Day) JM was strafing Japanese held Hengyang airfield, formerly a USAAF base. His P-51B was hit by ground fire in the coolant system and his engine quit on a 500 MPH low pass at gun emplacements. Over the middle of the field about a thousand feet high, three more explosive shells hit right outside his windshield. He was able to glide away from the field maybe a mile and bailed out at a hazardous 300 feet. He landed beside his burning plane and his chute drifted over his broken Mustang like a shroud. He threw his chute and all escape equipment into the fire and turned to run but was immediately met by a squad of Japanese soldiers. Thus began his status as a prisoner of war, a POW. The 75th "Flying Tiger Sharks" lost four brand new Mustangs that day: one pilot was killed, two walked back and JM was captured. The Japanese lost about twenty-five planes, in the air and on the ground, on that raid.

A Chinese soldier guards a line of American P-40 fighter planes, painted with the shark-face emblem of the "Flying Tigers."

—*Courtesy of National Archives*

After capture and walking back to the airfield, JM was tied to a tree with his hands behind him and he sat on the damp ground until late afternoon. All day he witnessed what he thought was the digging of his grave because it was believed the Japs usually shot their captured pilots. But the war was going badly for their military and their atrocities were slowing somewhat due to their "thoughts" of military reprisals.

His shoes were tied around his neck and hands remained tied behind his back. Then he was paraded barefoot through the streets of Hengyang for hours. He met Japanese military and Chinese civilians. The Japs were cruel and he was spat upon, knocked down with the flat side of a saber, hit in the head with a thrown horse shoe, cuffed about and otherwise physically abused. He was taken to a room where several Japanese pilots were and they had great sport over JM's plight. It was very humiliating and dehumanizing. Finally, he was laid down in a small cold room on a hard surface. He was aroused at daylight and untied for the first time in twenty hours. He was allowed to wash his face in freezing water. "When I saw my face in a metal mirror I didn't recognize my reflection. There was dried blood, mucus, bruises and extensive swelling. My hands looked like inflated rubber gloves from having been tied for so long".

A week later, JM was flown to Hankow and put in a half basement jail cell in a three storied brick building that housed some kind of headquarters. That was solitary confinement and JM did not accept it well. He was very unruly and began to beat on the door demanding that his shoes be given back and yelling if there were other prisoners there. It so happened that there were three others down the hall and one said, "Be quiet". He knew the penalty for being disruptive. JM settled down after he was placed in restraints for a few days. A heavy belt was fastened around his waist and his hands were cuffed to that.

Solitary confinement was very hard for JM since he tends to be extroverted but he had some comfort knowing that he was not alone. One interesting aspect of that time was a guard, unfit for combat, that JM called PIG EYE. Pig Eye was roley poley and his eyes were exceptionally slanted, thus the name. He was very harsh toward JM but the cells were not accessible by the guards. It seems Pig Eye antagonized Taylor every way he could but oddly JM figured a way to defeat each attempt. The masonry cells had solid wooden doors with a slit 12 X 1 inch about eye high. That was the only way to see in or out. Pig Eye would sneak up and jab his bayonet through this slit hoping to hit JM in the eyes. JM lay in wait once and when the blade came plunging in JM grabbed it and jammed it hard against the wood. Pig Eye had the short end and quickly became JM's victim. He couldn't get the bayonet back. JM reveled in the victory and began taunting the helpless guard. It was obvious both could be in serious trouble so JM let it go. Later, Pig Eye would open the 6 X 6 inch door at the bottom where the slop (food) was shoved in twice daily. He had gotten a 2 X 2 inch stick about seven feet long and would jab Taylor while he slept. Pig Eye had to get on his knees to do this. Sometimes PE would throw rocks in at JM. Again JM lay in wait and when the stick came in he took it away from the hapless Pig Eye. He stood it in the corner of his cell and it remained there until they were moved out. Another guard, "Beefu Stakee", was friendlier and would chat with JM in sign language and sounds. He even smuggled in an extra blanket to Taylor. He asked to borrow JM's flying gloves to wear to town one night. The gloves were returned the next day.

Once a week an officer would come down to unlock the cells and the prisoners were allowed out for five minutes; they had to empty the "latrine" (a wooden bucket which set in the corner of each 8 X 6 foot cell. The prisoners were allowed to wash their face in cold water and brush their teeth with a tooth brush which hung on the outside of the cell; it was used by each occupant of the cell.

One night part of a B-29 crew was brought in and they were very cold; one kid was crying. They said they were being sent to Japan the next day. After the war it was discovered they were all shot and their remains, including some dog tags, were discovered. The co-pilot of that plane, Vernon L. Schaeffer, ended up with us and was one of "The Diddled Dozen". This is a true story and I received a questionnaire from the War Department.

Solitary lasted almost two months and the four Americans were taken to the river docks where they met two other POW flyers. The six were transported by riverboat to Nanking; the boat ran by night and the POWs were held in a jail by day. Then they were transported by train to Shanghai. They were trucked out to Kiangwan POW camp where they met three more recent captives. The camp of 1100 was primarily made up of Wake Island survivors, Marines and civilians, the entire compliment of the North China US Embassy guard which included some Navy corpsmen and three doctors. Plus, the crew of an Italian ship that had scuttled their ship in the harbor and a few previously captured USAAF men made up the camp. This camp was more bearable than solitary but the airmen were kept under guard and separate from all other POWs. Other captured pilots joined them and the number grew to seventeen, five airmen and twelve officers. This was normal Jap POW fare with a continuous string of guards around the clock. Typical American youth gave them nick names. The Formosan: Smiley was friendly and bootlegged items to us at great risk to himself. He asked us to hide him from the Japs when the Americans came. Joe College, amiable and pleasant, Joe Palooka, carefree, Moon Mullins, Tiny Tim AND The Arkansas Traveler, stern, hateful, despicable Jap Sgt. Always stomping in his quick walk and saber rattling.

As the war went badly for Japan, the Japanese government decided to move the POWs to Japan. Obviously, they wanted something with which to barter in case of defeat. This trip was literally hell for the POW's. They were loaded into box cars and stuffed together like cattle. First, they were shipped by freight trains to Peking then up through Manchuria and down Korea to Fusan. After being deloused, they were disembarked onto a small cargo ship for the thirty six hour hazardous trip across the Korean Straight to Honshu Island, Japan. They were loaded onto a passenger train that went through the major cities on the east coast and passed through Tokyo on July 4, 1945.

After more hustle and bustle and a ferry ride across to Hokkaido Island on July 6, 1945 they ended up on the Japanese Imperial Army Northern Headquarters grounds near Sapporo. Only the twelve pilots were sent there and being disappointed, they named themselves "The Diddled Dozen". Once again they shared one room with full time guard on duty. Rations were very limited and Japan was being closed in by U.S. Forces. The war was winding down and Harry Truman "bravely" dropped the A bombs twice. Japan capitulated and things immediately got better for The Diddled Dozen. The Japs turned on the hospitality and wined and dined them daily. After four days of expecting a B-29 to make a drop, a note was dropped from one tied to a wrench for weight and trailing a red life raft sail. The note was written on a navigational chart of the area and read as follows:

"Hi Fellows: We will be back as soon as possible with supplies. We know you need them and are doing our best.
500th Bomb Group.
Major Vance E. Black"

Rations dropped by B-29s finally reached them from another location. The Diddled Dozen was recovered by USAAF on September 12, 1945, a month after the surrender. JM Taylor landed in San Francisco on October 16, 1945.

JM tried to reach Major Black years later and found out that he died in a North Korean POW camp. JM Taylor still has the parachute and the chart with the hand written note by Major Black. It will probably be in a museum someday.

TONY MUSCARELLA,SOUTHAVEN,MS.LANDING AT IWO JIMA FEB.19,1945.
HES CARRING A M ` 3006 Machine Gun,Ml Carbine,45 AUTO,& 2 K-Bar.
JOINED USMC MAY 1942,Age 14,Discharged May 1946 Aage 18,HE WAS
17 in Dec 1944.Youngest USMC to See Combat WW2,& Wounded 1943.
TONY DIED JAN,20,1995 Age 67.30 Days before Iwo s 50th Adv.

Tony Muscarella
(Iwo Jima- 1945)
—*Courtesy of Dino's Restaurant*

Nick White - 1944
(on right)
—*Courtesy of Nick White*

CHAPTER VII
THE CAPTURE OF IWO JIMA

Story of Nick White
and Tony Muscarella

ON D-DAY, FEBRUARY 19, 1945, TONY MUSCARELLA LANDED with the 4th Marine Division on Iwo Jima. He can still be viewed on official Marine film coming on the beach with his machine gun over his right shoulder. Joe Rosenthal (the famous A.P. photographer of the flag on Mount Surabachi) was on Tony's landing craft. On February 21, 1945 (D-Day + 2) Nick White landed on Iwo Jima with the 3rd Marine Division. His division backed up the 4th and 5th divisions that had landed with Tony.

The 4th and 5th had taken enormous casualties from the 27,000 Japanese defenders. The Japanese dug under the island and created an enormous tunneled fortress of caves, bunkers, 5" thick concrete pill boxes and 11 miles of underground passageways. Army Air Force photos had not reveled the webs of catacombs to the Navy and Marine pre-invasion planners. The Navy had amassed a huge invasion fleet of over 450 vessels. The 4th and 5th Marine Divisions were slated to take the island. The 3rd division was in reserve for the invasion of Japan's home islands.

The island is roughly five miles long and 25 miles at its widest point. It is shaped like a lamb chop. Iwo Jima has black ash beaches.

Nick White's 3rd Marine Division loaded up their landing craft on D-Day + 1. They couldn't land because of the enormous amount of damaged, wrecked, or sunken landing craft close to the beach. The dry beach was also covered with hundreds of dead marines wrapped in body bags or in Navy/ Marine rain ponchos.

The Japanese Lieutenant General Tadamichi Kuribayashi had changed their fighting strategy. This type of fighting was different from Tinian, Saipan, and Guam. He asked each Japanese soldier to kill at least 10 Marines before dying for their Emperor. Their death oath was engraved on

the Kuribayashi sword. Before Iwo Jima, the Americans had overwhelmed the best Japanese troops (both regular army and imperial marines). The American military had awesome battlefield firepower which humiliated the Japanese military. The underground fortress at Iwo Jima was a challenge for our tough and brave young marines.

6,821 Americans died in this battle, the heaviest in Marine Corps history. Only 1,051 Japanese surrendered of their 27,000 defenders.

Tony Muscarella had great "night vision". His eyes dilated better than those of his comrades in the 4th marine division. He was a member of the 4th's 25th Marine Combat Regiment. He was a well trained

Tony Muscarella (speaking to children at a school, later on in his life)
—*Courtesy of Dino's Restaurant*

machine gunner and sharp shooter. By D-day plus 2 he was needed to kill night time Japanese snipers. His fellow Marines would come to get him in the middle of the night and ask him if he would eliminate the pests. He could see the enemy, but his fellow marines couldn't.

Tony was in a large 4th Division trench early one morning with other marines one of which was wounded. Sixty to Seventy Japanese made a "screaming banzai attack" in the early twilight. Their colonel breached the Marine defenses and got into the trench next to Tony and the wounded Marine. There was a hand to hand struggle between Tony and the Japanese Colonel. The Colonel almost killed the wounded marine with the Samurai sword that he was wielding. Tony shot him, point blank, in the head with his 45 caliber pistol. After the attack, Tony extracted a gold tooth from the Colonel's mouth in addition to keeping his Samurai sword. This tooth was to become Tony's good luck symbol. It was considered to be like a rabbit's foot. He showed it to me once. He always carried it in his right pants pocket. Another friend of mine told me his father was on a P.T. Boat circling Iwo Jima during the battle. He was only a baby at this time. His mother received a leather pouch for him, with a baby rattler that contained Japanese teeth inside to rattle.

Nick White
—*Courtesy of Nick White*

The ferocity of the battle inspired our brave marines to learn from the Native Americans among them. The Navajo code talkers were present with three Marine divisions. "Howling Mad" Smith was the commander of the 3rd, 4th, and 5th divisions.

Water was a problem for the Marines. Nick White relates the story of the problems the 3rd division had with bathing. After the 3rd, 4th, and 5th Divisions pushed the Japanese back and captured the first Japanese fighter airfield, the 3rd decided to wash up. However, no clean water was available on this tiny volcanic island. The Navy gave each marine a two gallon tin can of water to take a sponge bath. Nick White and two of his buddies were sitting on a make shift bench while sponge bathing. A Japanese sniper shot his pal in the head with a 22 caliber rifle. The unlucky Marine had been sitting in the middle. It could have easily been Nick.

One day, Nick was in a Japanese mortar attack on the 3rd Division. It caused Nick and a buddy to jump into a foxhole. His Sergeant Major came around later and fussed about them still being in the foxhole. Minutes later, the Japanese mortars let loose another barrage and the Sergeant Major jumped into the foxhole. He turned to Nick and said that they were very smart marines.

Tony Muscarella has left us but he wrote a book about his experiences on Iwo Jima. The book is called *Iwo Jima the Young Heroes*.

Nick White is a college professor teaching young law students at the University of Memphis. He is Dean Emeritus of the University Of Memphis Law School.

Linkwood Williams

—Courtesy of Linkwood Williams

CHAPTER VIII
THE TUSKEGEE AIRMAN

Story of Dr. Linkwood Williams

DR. WILLIAMS WAS GOING TO COLLEGE AT THE TUSKEGEE Institute. He also worked his way through school as a part time maintenance man. One day, he was observing the Tuskegee Flyers and was quite impressed and decided to join them and drop out of school. Dr. Williams later went to pilot school and became an instructor as well as Daniel "Chappie" James (the first four star black general). The federal program that they used was CPT (Civilian Pilot Training). It was offered in college around 1939 and 1940 because the United States was preparing for World War II. Hitler was rattling his swords.

The Tuskegee Airmen were Army Air force, black fighter pilots that flew bomber B-17 escort duty. The German Luftwaffe was still active in 1944 and 1945. They had some jets and also an advanced Messerschmitt 109, which they called the "Tunk". The Tuskegee Airmen flew P-40's, P-47's, and P-51's against the German planes. The P-51 was the best American plane that they used. The Germans feared it and called it the "Jug". It was a tank killer and the best of the best.

Two Tuskegee Airmen sunk a stacked German destroyer by shooting machine guns into it. It had munitions on its deck. What a bit of pure American luck!

The B-17 pilots did not want Tuskegee airmen to escort them at first, but after they heard about their prowess in the air they asked them to come along. The Tuskegee Airmen's P-51's had their propeller head

Linkwood Williams
—Courtesy of Linkwood Williams

and tail painted red for recognition. The main planes that they shot down were the Messerschmitt 109's and Fokker 90's.

An exciting event in Dr. Williams's air career was when he saw Eleanor Roosevelt, getting into a plane at the Tuskegee Airfield. She backed the black airmen one hundred percent and helped with inspiration. Her support and our brave president, Harry Truman, integrated our armed services in 1946, he did not ask anybody, he just took action and did it himself.

Dr. Linkwood Williams
—*Courtesy of Linkwood Williams*

Linkwood met his wife at the Tuskegee Airbase. She was working as a secretary for the Army Air Corp. He would stop by and wave at her through the window on his way to work. He would wave at her until she waved back.

Dr. Linkwood Williams is a retired OBGYN in Memphis. He has attended some of his reunions. He attended one in 2000, in San Antonio, where he received the Coveted Heritage Award. He also attended another reunion the following year, 2001 in Memphis.

Norma and Wesley Rogers

—Courtesy of Norma Rogers

CHAPTER IX
3RD ARMY- BOOTS ON THE GROUND

Story of Wesley Rogers
and Norma Rogers

NORMA MY FRIND AT church

NORMA ROGERS IS THE WIDOW OF WESLEY ROGERS, a WWII 3rd Army veteran. Norma attended Vassar College in New York. She was a member of the Vassar College Choir. The choir sang for President and Mrs. Franklin Delano Roosevelt in 1939. The place was the Roosevelts' Hyde Park residence. Some Norwegian royalty were visiting the Roosevelts. The "Winds of War" were blowing in Europe, and FDR was keeping abreast by these personal social visits.

Norma met Wesley in 1939 after her family had moved to Cordova, then a small town outside of Memphis, TN. Wesley and Norma met at a festive Christmas party. She was a junior at Vassar College at that time. They were later married at his army camp at Fort Eustis, VA.

In January 1944, after a sea voyage aboard the famous Queen Elizabeth I, Wesley landed in Glasgow, Scotland. Wesley's unit ended up a member of Patton's Third Army. He was in the famous 411th AAA Gun Battalion. On the 9th of June 1944, Wesley's unit landed at Utah Beach. They were signaled with thumbs up by the 101st Airborne troops who were guarding the beach's perimeter. The 101st Airborne troops needed, for their protection, the big 90mm guns that the AAA Gun Battalion used. The 90mm could be tilted up to guard bridges from German Messerschmitt 109's. It also could be tilted down to destroy German Panzer and Panther tanks. What a weapon!

From June of 1944 through the Fall of 1944: Wesley Rogers's unit moved inland to help coordinate ground troop-air defenses. His first assignment was defending Ste. Mère Église. His outfit shot at 77 German planes in combat there. Wesley was in France for the following battles: The Hedge Rows, The Breakout at Avranches, and The Fire Storm at the Seine River, during the Battle for Paris. The Americans captured more Germans in France than the Russians did at Stalingrad.

"Many received Christmas cards"
—*Courtesy of The Lightning: The History of the 78th Infantry Division*

During December of 1944, at The Battle of the Bulge, Wesley Rogers's unit guarded the bridge that Third Army used to reach Bastogne. Third Army had to make a 90 degree turn in December 1944 to move northwest across the bridge towards Bastogne. This was his most important responsibility during the war when he guarded the bridge that 3rd Army needed to go north and relieve the 101st Airborne, who were totally surrounded at the town of Bastogne. On December 26, 1944, 3rd Army tank commander Creighton Abrams relieved Bastogne and cut a wide open supply corridor to the city.

For forty days and forty nights Wesley and his combat troops were affected by the unusually cold weather. Many times Wesley stayed up all night; he was alerted of approaching aircraft by army radar. His anti-aircraft guns performed well against the best German dive bombers. He wrote many of his letters to Norma while on long hours of duty during the night. Wesley's unit also guarded George Patton's Third Army Headquarters in Luxemburg and Germany. All in all, the 411th AAA Gun Battalion unit was in the thick of fighting and shot down many German planes. They were decorated for outstanding service.

Even at the end of the war, Wesley's unit helped at Dachau Concentration Camp. The barbarian acting Reinhard Heydrich was in charge of Dachau where he performed unconscionable acts against civilians. War is hell, and the atrocities perpetrated by German soldiers were unbelievable. Jews, Catholics, innocent Belgian children, Belgian adult civilians, captured Polish, Russian, and American soldiers were all executed by Hitler's SS Troopers during the battle for Europe. American troops did retaliate for this bestiality. On the Russian front, the German Army and Russian Army did not use any of the Geneva Convention Rules of War. Bestiality is the most accurate description for the savage behavior used by some units of the German troops that were transferred from the Russian front during The Battle of the Bulge.

Back in the USA Norma Rogers worked at a radio station while Wesley was in service. She was a newscaster and disc jockey for WMFD in Wilmington, North Carolina. Norma explained to me the meaning of the words "boots on the ground"[1]. It applies to anyone following a

---

1 "The sergeant I'm still writing to at a hospital in Texas is currently "boots on the ground" with his buddies who are still in Iraq although both of his feet were blown off (up to the knee) and he's permanently out of action." – Dr. Norma P. Rogers

campaign from a distance and emotionally. Relating to her experience, it simply meant following her loved one's invasion route across France and Germany during World War II. Personal letters and newspapers helped Norma locate Wesley's "boots on the ground".

Welsey and Norma Rogers

—*Courtesy of Norma Rogers*

Wesley's family settled in Shelby County in 1837. They originally owned a large hunk of this county that contained Memphis. He was raised on a dairy farm near Cordova, TN. He and Norma lived in Cordova after the war. Wesley was recognized by the town of Cordova for his bravery and leadership during World War II. We all miss him, but his spirit still lives among us. Let us never forget the sacrifices his generation made to insure the world's freedom of speech and democracy. God bless the World War II veterans and their descendants.

Karl Leonhard

—Courtesy of Inge and Gabrielle Leonhard

CHAPTER X
1940-1945

Story of Karl Leonhard:
A German Flying Ace

INGE LEONHARD, KARL'S WIDOW, TOLD ME THE EVENTS that are included in this short story. I interviewed her twice and the following is The Way it Was.

Karl Leonhard flew in combat during the entire duration of WWII. The last two years of WWII, for the German Luftwaffe, was a long and arduous ordeal.

Beginning from the very first day of WWII up until the very last day Karl Leonhard was never shot down. He made three belly landings after almost five years of combat flying. That is why I call him a German Ace!

Karl came up through the ranks in his five years of flying starting out just as a pilot and became Squadron Leader of the **Pik-Ass (Spielkarte)** or "Ace of Spades" Luftwaffe. Later on towards the end of the war he was promoted to Group Commander. A Group Commander was head of a combination of four squadrons.

Karl escorted German bombers towards their targets and back from raids over England. He flew combat missions over North Africa, Sicily, Italy, Germany, and France. He did very little flying on the Eastern front. Karl was mostly a Western front Messerschmitt 109 flyer. Inge, his wife, said the best plane he ever flew was the **Tank 152**, pronounced "tunk". It was named after the man who developed it, Professor Tank. It was propeller driven, (not a jet), very fast and these were the planes they were using towards the end of the war.

Karl Leonhard
—*Courtesy of Inge and Gabrielle Leonhard*

During the Battle of France in June of 1940 he flew the Messerschmitt 109's. He was assigned to attack British Spitfires first, then their tanks and then their artillery. In June of 1940 the German army broke through the French 7th Army and opened up a 40 to 50 mile wide path that could not be closed. The German Army moved very quickly towards Paris. The reason why the French lost the war is they simply had no reserves to plug up the hole. The British Expeditionary Force created a major miracle and escaped from Dunkirk, France by ship and boat to England.

After France surrendered, Inge Leonhard stayed in Germany. She was a chemist who had graduated from a special German school before WWII.

Karl was later stationed in France to escort the German bombers to England during the blitz of 1940 and 1941. He attacked the British Spitfires.

After that assignment, they promoted him and switched his assignment. They wanted him to protect France and Germany from British and American long- range bombers, so Karl was switched from escort work to the defense of France and Germany. The British and American long-range bombers were pounding their cities, manufacturing plants and rail yards. This went on throughout 1943 and 1944.

Karl Leonhard
—*Courtesy of Inge and Gabrielle Leonhard*

Karl Leonhard
—*Courtesy of Inge and Gabrielle Leonhard*

After the Battle of the Bulge started on December 16, 1944, he was mostly used to defend Berlin and the German cities from the heavy bombing by the American and British planes. The British bombed at night. The Americans bombed during the day.

As Karl took off on his last mission, he viewed Hitler's plane still on the runway at Berlin. Karl flew his squadron to Denmark and surrendered to the British. This was the day before Germany surrendered to the Allies.

As he landed in the very Northern tip of Germany right near Denmark, his mind tumbled back to the five years of hell he just went through as a German Ace Messerschmitt 109 pilot. He remembered the days during 1940, the victorious Battle of France and those attacks on the British Expeditionary Force. The taste of glory - what a fleeting moment!

A rumor was out that the American General Patton would not stop, he wanted to keep going; (here in America we thought he was going

Karl Leonhard

—Courtesy of Inge and Gabrielle Leonhard

to push the Russians back because he didn't like them). The rumor in Germany was that British General Montgomery would not stop and was going to keep going and push the Russians back where they should be. Hearing this rumor, some of the Germans wanted to turn their planes over to the British but it was only a rumor. Karl landed and was taken P.O.W. by the British.

This may be the only account of this veteran's experiences. With the cold war heating up in Europe, with an opportunistic, pioneer spirit,

Inge and Karl came to the states after the war to start their lives over. They didn't bring any literature or memorabilia from the war with them when they came here. They were ready to start a complete new life. Inge helped develop latex paint when she came to the U.S.A. Inge and Karl have a daughter, Gabriella, a marketer and exquisite producer of Napa Valley wines called Vertex, Juxtaposition, and Equilateral.

Adolph Hitler and Benito Mussolini
—Courtesy of National Archives

Bob Shafer—Hollandia, New Guinea, 1944

—*Courtesy of Bob Shafer*

CHAPTER XI
THE ARMY ENGINEER
Story of Robert Shafer

AFTER COMPLETING TWO YEARS IN THE COLLEGE OF Engineering at UT Knoxville, Bob entered the army, taking basic training at Keesler Field in Biloxi, MS. After basic, he was transferred to a pre-meteorology program at Vanderbilt University. After the program was shut down, he was transferred to the Airborne Engineer Training Center at Richmond, Virginia, only to find that program also closed. He was then transferred to Geiger Field at Spokane, Washington, where he was assigned to the 1892nd Engineer Aviation Battalion. After maneuvers at Yakima, Washington and in the Bitteroot Mountains in Idaho, the unit was sent overseas to Hollandia, Dutch New Guinea. After several months there the unit was sent to Ie Shima, a small island off the west coast of Okinawa in the Ryukyu Island group. The island was about two miles wide and five miles long and was tiered like a wedding cake. It was composed of mostly coral. The island was taken by units of the 77th Infantry Division. Ernie Pyle, the famous war correspondent was killed on Ie Shima. The battalion was transported from New Guinea on five LSTs. The one carrying Bob's company had over one thousand steel drums of gasoline on the tank deck. This gasoline was being taken from a rear area to the Ryukyu Islands which were a forward area. "When we reached the Ryukyu Island group we put into a harbor at an island called Kerama Rhetto for landing instructions. That afternoon we were hit by a series of Kamakazi attacks in which one ship, an LSM, was sunk and a large seaplane tender was struck and set on fire but did not sink. The attacks continued all through the night.

Ie Shima was bombed regularly by the Japanese, with about 180 attacks in one three month period. Often, however, only one plane got through due to the night fighters which intercepted the flights of bombers and downed many of them.

Ie was to be a launching pad for some of the air cover for the invasion of Japan, being home to B-24s, B-25s, P-38s, P-51s, P-47s, a few Corsairs, and even a few P-61s.

There was no fresh water on the island, with the drinking and cooking water being furnished by evaporators. Later, wells were drilled on the island which provided water suitable for bathing but not drinking. A lot of the time, troops caught rain water off the tents in their helmets and used it for bathing.

Once, while making a survey on a part of the island still threatened by Japanese holdouts hiding in the caves, Bob's survey party was fired upon from the caves. They knew that there were Japanese in the area, having been warned by an infantry patrol and others. The only one who was armed was Bob, and when the shots rang out the group hit the dirt behind a large rock and when the dust settled, Bob was on the bottom of the stack and his weapon was under him. A Lieutenant wandered up and commented about Bob taking a break, at which time the shots came again, the Lt. said he would take a break too and after a while they all pealed off and got out of there, with Bob, being the last to go and as the party chief, he grabbed up the surveying instrument and his weapon and they all left that place in a hurry.

The 1892nd was one of several engineer battalions on Ie Shima and together they built three air strips along with taxiways, parking areas, etc. They were building the fourth strip when the war ended. There was also, "SeaBees" on the island. Their work was mostly in the harbor and shipping facilities. The "SeaBees" lived pretty good, having a Quonset hut for a recreation hall, complete with a pool table and coke machines.

The night the Japanese announced their surrender, Ie Shima was bombed by a single Japanese airplane. Bob learned later that it was flown by a colonel who was against the surrender and in a fit or rage, had his plane armed and fueled for one "last hurrah." However, between the time we dropped the atom bombs and the Japanese announced their surrender, the 1892nd feared that they would be subject to gas attacks. They cleaned out their gas masks which had been neglected for a long time. In addition, they had a series of 1 x 6 boards about two feet long and attached to a short stake driven into the ground and painted with a special paint which would bubble up in the presence of poison gas. There was an old steel wheel, or other metal with a steel rod handle which was to be rung in the event of a gas attack. Fortunately, there was no gas attack.

After the war ended, the 1892nd moved over to Okinawa and set up an asphalt plant. They started putting asphalt pavement over the existing coral runway at Kadena Airfield. I understand that Kadena is still an active airbase for our troops on Okinawa. By the end of December, 1945, most of the original members of the unit

Anne and Bob Shafer
—*Courtesy of Bob Shafer*

were on their way back to the USA for discharge at various discharge centers located near their homes.

"Tag" Weldon

CHAPTER XII
THE NAVY HELLCAT PILOT

Story of W.K. "Tag" Weldon

"TAG" WAS TRAINED TO FLY AT VARIOUS NAVAL AIR BASES including: Millington, Tennessee, Corpus Christi, Texas, and Melbourne, Florida. He learned how to practice carrier landing on two ships called The Sable and The Wolverine. The Sable and The Wolverine were converted side-wheelers. They were simulated to be practice aircraft carriers in that they had an aircraft carrier type platform built onto their decks. At that time "Tag" was stationed at the Great Lakes naval station near Chicago, Illinois where he practiced landing many times on the two carrier type ships. The Sable and The Wolverine always plied the waters of Lake Michigan near Chicago.

"Tag" usually landed at 110 miles per hour. A hook and a wire stopped him and the wind direction and speed of the ship was a definite factor in a safe landing. A Landing Signal Officer, (L.S.O.), always waived the carrier based planes in to properly land. The L.S.O. had bright red or orange paddles that signaled the pilot if he was landing correctly or incorrectly. "Tag" was sometimes waived away if he was too low, too high, or coming in too fast.

"Tag" became a Navy Hellcat pilot. A throat microphone was used by all Hellcat pilots. A pilot could warn his partner pilot that a Japanese fighter plane was coming in at four o'clock or six o'clock. Also, no idle chatter was allowed on the throat microphones.

"Tag" had a scare while flying with a Navy Instructor at the Naval Base in Millington, TN. They were flying upside-down in a "yellow peril" training plane, (also known as the N3N), when they got into an upside-down spin. The instructor bailed out of the wrong side of the plane and got hit by the plane. "Tag" jumped out of the correct side of the plane in the spin and wasn't hit. Unfortunately, his parachute did not open correctly until he was almost 300 feet from the ground. "Tag" survived by landing in a tree. His instructor was not so lucky and did not make it.

"Tag" first sailed on The Bunker Hill but was transferred over to the larger aircraft carrier called The Essex. The Essex was known to "wreak havoc" wherever she sailed. "Tag" destroyed three Japanese fighters when the Essex attacked the main Japanese fighter base at Manila in the Philippians. He caught one Japanese plane in the air and fired his machine guns. The other two Japanese planes were taxing down the runway. "Tag" told me he made a swooping pass at them and gave them a squirt of his Hellcat's machineguns.

The Essex attacked the Japanese fighter base at Okinawa. "Tag" said the Essex was near Iwo Jima at the time. They topped all their gas tanks and they flew 50 to 100 feet above the Pacific Ocean until they reached Okinawa. Then they climbed to 3500 feet to make a diving attack. "Tag's" friend Hubie Houston was shot down by the Japanese and captured. He spent the rest of the war in a P.O.W. camp with the famous WWII Ace pilot Gregory "Pappy" Boyington. Another friend, "Red" Gordon, was shot down and was picked up by an American Submarine. "Red" beat the Essex back to Pearl Harbor for rest and relaxation.

During the Battle of Okinawa, the Essex received a kamikaze direct hit on her port side. "Tag" was taking off at that same instant from the Essex and had to fly through the smoke and debris from the imploded kamikaze. The Essex landing deck was damaged and on returning to land from his mission, he was radioed that his flight of planes had to land on the nearby Ticonderoga Aircraft Carrier. The Essex was quickly repaired by the next day and ready to receive "Tag's" flight back.

"Tag" said that his air group from the Essex destroyed many Japanese shipping and land targets from the Philippians to Formosa, to Indo-China to Iwo Jima, and finally to Okinawa. The Essex also sunk a French Navy cruiser in the Harbor at Saigon Indo-China that had been captured by the Japanese Navy.

"Tag" said the Navy Hellcat could dive better and had more firepower and armament than the many Japanese type fighters. "Tag" said they used the "thatcher weave formation" against the Japanese. They would fly in a formation of two by two and use circles and figure eights to confuse the Japanese. If a Japanese plane got behind "Tag" and his partner, they would do figure eights. Then his partner would slow up and cut under the bottom of a figure eight to get behind the Japanese fighter and shoot it down.

"Tag" Weldon
—*Courtesy of Ann Weldon*

"Tag" has left us but, his spirit will always be with the future generations of Americans.

Sam Weintraub (top row, middle)

—*Courtesy of Jeff Weintraub*

CHAPTER XIII
JAPANESE HOLDOUTS: TINIAN ISLAND IN THE MARIANAS

Story of Sam Weintraub

"HELL, I'M NOT GOING TO KILL JAPS JUST FOR THE HELL of it!" These are the words of the American General that gave Sam Weintraub the go ahead to secure Tinian Island in the Mariana's. His name was General Von Kimble and he spoke those words at a general staff meeting while discussing The Japanese Surrender Campaign.

Sam Weintraub was able to save many lives on both sides. As Island G2, (Security Head Officer), Sam instituted the "surrender patrols" that had great success.

The Navy supplied a Destroyer that broadcast surrender pleas on loudspeakers to the Japanese holdouts that were in caves along the Tinian coastline. A Cub plane circled the island and radioed the Japanese cave activities coming and going to Sam on the Destroyer.

Sam recalled that during the finale' of the battle for Tinian, the Japanese Commander of Tinian, General Kakuta, committed Hari Kari, (a form of suicide considered by the Japanese to be honorable). There were also 1,000 plus civilians and 100 Japanese soldiers perched on a suicide cliff on the Southern end of the Island. The Japanese soldiers had been jumping one at a time. The Marines were closing in on them. The Japanese blew up 30 civilians with dynamite and a large majority of civilians stampeded down the hill from the cliff to join the Marines and safety.

The capture of the two Japanese soldiers by the names of Toughie and Standby helped Sam persuade other Japanese holdouts to surrender. The two of them would go into the caves and talk the other Japanese holdouts into surrendering. Toughie had surrendered stark naked with a grenade in his hand. "The search and destroy Marines" had blasted him out of his cave.

Sam received an "emotional bath" on his return to Tinian in 1982. He also visited Japan in 1988 and 1989 and dined with Tinian civilians and Japanese veterans. The daughter of one civilian family that had committed suicide on Tinian visited with Sam in Japan. Her parents and her sister had jumped off the cliff but instead she ran down the hill and joined the Marines for safety.

Sam also had an encounter with a Japanese soldier whose name was Take Ko who threw a "dud hand grenade" on the top of his tent. Luckily, Sam watched it fizzle out instead of exploding.

One Japanese enlisted man named Daizaburo Ohyama wrote Sam a letter about how cruel his superior officer was and how the officer had tortured one of the brave American Navy pilots who was held captive. This pilot chose death over revealing information about the fleet. Sam searched in the Navy archives for this pilot but couldn't identify him from two others who were also shot down over Tinian. He tried to acquire that pilot's name or "dog tags" to help solve this mystery. Daizaburo was going to write the American pilot's family and tell them of his bravery.

Most of the material used here came from two of Sam's oral history interviews I had the pleasure to conduct in 1992. Unfortunately, Sam Weintraub is no longer with us but I am fortunate to have a copy of his memoirs and two thirty minute interviews. Sam was a very brave and compassionate man who tried to save lives and his noble spirit will be with our nation now and always.

Here is a journal, *Reunion in Tokyo*, that was written by Sam Weintraub.

Reunion in Tokyo:
Journal by Sam Weintraub

During the last year of World War II, I served as G2, General Staff, responsible for Intelligence and Security of the Island of Tinian in the Mariannas.

After a period of "search and destroy" patrols on the Island, we converted our group to efforts to persuade Japanese to surrender, sometimes venturing unarmed into caves for this purpose. We were able to save many lives on both sides. There was considerable national press and magazine coverage both during and after the war. (1945 Liberty magazine and 1958 Climax magazine articles enclosed).

In October, 1989, after searching for many years, I was able to locate and meet with some of the Japanese soldiers who had surrendered to us after hiding out in the jungles and caves of Tinian. This struck a chord in Japan; newspapers throughout Japan carried stories of the reunion and of the life-saving operation of Tinian (articles enclosed).

The reunion was deeply rewarding; the moving, nighttime shadows of Tinian emerged at the dinner table. Joy, warmth, emotion, storytelling and picture taking continued for hours. Former enemies filled in the gaps of incidents and actions, though the specific participants were unknown to each other at the time. . "Oh, my gosh, that wasn't you, was it?" was a feeling expressed many times throughout the day.

Unbelievable incidents were recounted, such as the officer who wouldn't surrender but sent me a bunch of bananas as a sign of trust: "To Major

Sam, all-conquering American Forces."! (He later came out). The officer had been the superior officer of one of the participants in the reunion, Hiroshi Morioka. Morioka and the others told me the officer was Lieutenant Maeda, second son of Count Maeda of a famous old Samurai family and still alive in Japan.

Another incident involved an officer whom we visited in a cave several times to persuade him to surrender but he refused. On one such visit, we learned that he was a major league baseball fan. Vince Smith, a catcher for the Pittsburgh Pirates, who was visiting the island with a USO group, agreed to go into the cave with an interpreter to talk to him. They talked baseball for over an hour and a half; the next night, the officer walked out on his own! We nicknamed him "moonlight," because he came out in the moonlight!

Daizaburo Ohyama, the Secretary-General of the Tinian Survivor group, who, along with Kenzo Sugiura, President of Brother Industries, U.S.A., of Memphis, Tennessee, organized the reunuion, said "Moonlight" was Lt. Otaka, his Commanding officer. Two others at our gathering had been in the cave with Otaka. They said he was a strict disciplinarian who for a long time had refused to let them surrender. In 1951, Lt. Otaka published a book concerning his experiences on Tinian. I had sent Ohyama copies of magazine articles of our adventures on Tinian, including the April, 1958 issue of Climax magazine which contained a picture of Lt. Otaka. In return Ohyama gave me a copy of a page from Otaka's book containing Otaka's picture, looking just as strict and martial as they described him. Otaka passed away before our reunion.

Another incident we shared involved a POW who wanted to rejoin his comrades still hiding in the hills. A U.S. Officer had allowed the POW to go back to the hills (with several days food supply). Morioka had been a friend of the POW and had tried to talk him out of going back. Morioka had been hoping to find out at our reunion who that officer was; he was astounded and gratified to learn that I was that officer! The POW came out again several days later bringing others with him. (See letter from Morioka).

The Japanese also recounted their desperate efforts to survive for many months, under incredible conditions, prior to their surrender. They recalled stealing food from the garbage dumps of U.S. troops risking their lives to do so, eating spaghetti which American troops had thrown over the sides of the cliffs, and similar incidents. They "complained" about the spaghetti: "Too sour!" they referred to out mass destruction of jungle to make room for B-29 runways as an intrusion into their "residential areas!" Although much was recalled with laughter, there was deep emotion shared over the past, and heartfelt sorrow for fallen comrades on both sides.

After we invaded Tinian, the Japanese ultimately were driven to a cliff at the southern tip of the island. They had over 10,000 Japanese civilians from the island with them. One by one the soldiers jumped off the cliff (Suicide Cliff). We pleaded with them with bullhorns to come down, that we wouldn't harm them, but they continued their tragic "parade," one by one; and refused to let the civilians, they separated a number of them and blew them up with dynamite. However, it had the opposite effect; the civilians stampeded down the cliff and were saved.

Mrs. Takae Ko, one of the civilian ladies I met during my stay in Tokyo at a separate reunion with Tinian civilians, was on that cliff with her mother and father and sister. Her father insisted that they jump off and he and her mother and sister jumped. She refused to jump and was there to meet with me in Tokyo! Mrs. Ko, a young girl at the time and now living in Yokohama, visits Tinian every year, but her 18-year-old can't comprehend the whole incident.

An exhilarating event in our surrender campaign was the use of a Destroyer to broadcast from open water to Japanese hiding out in caves in the cliffs at the water's edge, virtually inaccessible to us by land. This included the use of a cub plane circling overhead to spot and relay information to me on the ship of the movement of surrendering Japanese up the cliff so I could forewarn Marines in the area that these were friendly Japanese and not to shoot. We stationed interpreters at various points at the top of the cliffs; they would welcome the surrendering Japanese, quickly evaluate them and send out to the ship by picket boat any especially articulate and persuasive Japanese who would in turn address the Japanese they had just left behind.

Possibly the most gripping aspect of the destroyer incident was the desperate marshalling of arguments until far into the night by battle-hardened soldiers in my group, for my use to persuade the Commanding General and my fellow General Staff members to use the destroyer. Most of the General Staff couldn't understand why we just didn't "kill the Japs." However, we were convinced of the military efficiency of a surrender campaign. Just as important to us, we had to kill too many Japanese soldiers who might have surrendered but for the abruptness of our combat confrontations with them. And worse yet, some of the dead turned out to be innocent civilians.

The decisive meeting with the General Staff on the surrender campaign and the use of the Destroyer ended abruptly as I was expounding on the military basis of the surrender operation; the General interrupted me to say, "Hell, I'm not going to kill the Japs just for the hell of it!" For a man with these sentiments he had the improbable name of General Frederick Von Kimble!

Some of the participants in our reunion were in those caves and heard our broadcasts though they didn't come out at that time.

The commanding General of the Japanese forces on Tinian was General Kakuta, who at the end committed Hari Ki (suicide). His daughter missed our reunion; she had gone back to the General's village in Kiusho where a ceremony in his memory took place the day of the reunion. I hope to meet with her and other Tinian connections at a future time in Japan.

I was happy to yield a good part of my picture collection to my new friends as they excitedly poured through the pictures and found Tinian comrades.

The reunion in Japan was the culmination of a decade-long search for the Japanese POWs with whom I worked in the surrender campaign, particularly their leaders whom we nicknamed Toughie and Standby. After considerable research and correspondence, I concluded that some of these POWs might have remained on the Island after the war and I traveled to Tinian in 1982 to try to find them. However, I found that they had all been sent back to Japan within a year after the war ended. Please see the Memphis Commercial Appeal article enclosed, "Sam Weintraub's Search."

Still searching, I visited Japan in April 1988; the story of that prior visit along with pictures of Toughie and Standby was also published throughout Japan. Among other responses, I received a sad but beautiful letter (copy enclosed) from Daizaburo Ohyama the leader of the Tinian Survivor Group in Japan, mentioned earlier.

In his letter, Ohyama tells the moving story of a downed U.S. Navy pilot, captured by Ohyama's unit, who chose torture and death over revealing information. Ohyama tells of his "long time dream... somehow to let his family know... how brave (the pilot) was "and asked for my help in finding the family.

Through the good offices of Rear Admiral Jim Cossey, then Chief of Naval Air training at Millington Air Base, near Memphis, I was able to research the incident at the Naval Historical Center in Washington. I found 19 incidents of damaged or drowned planes in and around Tinian. Finally, we narrowed it down to 3 possible planes and their pilots who were missing in action in and around Tinian. However, efforts to pinpoint the particular pilot are thus far inconclusive for among other reasons concern about causing undue pain to surviving families by involving at least two of them prematurely. See Memorandum dated September 14, 1989.

My visit to Tinian in 1982 also had a strong emotional impact on the natives of the Island (Chomoros), who looked at me as a second McArthur. They had been shipped off to other islands by the Japanese before the war and they or their descendants were brought back by the U.S. after the war. They couldn't get enough of the story of how their Island was retaken from someone who was there and who was in a position of responsibility at that time.

* * * *

I have many pictures of our reunion as well as of our adventures on Tinian, including pictures of the Japanese POWs we worked with and others that surrendered to us, including wartime pictures of incidents involving Ohyama and others that I met with in Tokyo, which understandably bowled them over when they saw them. There are pictures of how it all started, Toughie and his friends being blasted out of their hideout and of Toughie leading the group up the side of the cave to surrender, stark naked, a grenade in his hand which we detected and forcibly removed! (Morioka informed us that he had left that cave the day before and had watched from a hideout 70 yards away). Toughie subsequently became our chief intermediary with the Japanese still holding out in the caves.

I have the names, addresses and telephone numbers of the Japanese soldiers with whom

I was reunited in Japan and of civilians in a separate reunion and many other pictures and memorabilia of Tinian and of my extended search, even including articles about our psychological activities in the Israeli Army Weekly and Israeli newspapers!

Perhaps of most importance, I kept a daily diary of the extraordinary and sometimes tragic events in the initial efforts to find and destroy the enemy and in our later happier surrender campaign.

Summary 2
(7/1/91)

ADDENDUM 1

The Atom Bomb group which bombed Hiroshima and Nagasaki was stationed on our Island.

Two days before the bombing of Hiroshima a friend and I were at dinner with Paul Tibbets, pilot of the Enola Gay, his navigator, his wing commander Col. Jim Davies (promoted to General the day of the bombing) and others at their mess, prior to a poker game. At one point, Davies, who was a couple of sheets to the wind, got up, held up his glass and looking at my friend and me said, "Gentleman, I want to drink a toast to a bomb, ten of which will end the war with Japan!" Although he had already said too much, he didn't go any further. We knew that they had an unusual weapon, but their security was so tight that despite my function as Island G-2, responsible for security on the Island, and despite "bribing" of the security officer of the bomb Group by taking him along on several of our surrender patrols, I was never able to learn exactly what it was until after the bomb went off. (We had a number of other extraordinary experiences involving the bomb).

Summary 2

ADDENDUM II

My diary also relates events of our earlier "search and destroy" patrolling and the later surrender campaign, some of which today seem as extraordinary as those recounted above. Yet I had perhaps even more unique experiences earlier on other Pacific Islands, some foreshadowing the human element of the surrender campaign, and one of which upon the culmination of an expeditionary force mission in the Ellice Island led to an air force commendation as the "inspiration" of the entire mission.

In 1943, as a young Lieutenant, I was assigned responsibility for 400 air support men who were temporarily attached to the 3rd Assron, which took over and developed the Ellice Islands south of the Gilbert Islands as bases for the bombing of Tarawa in the Gilbert Islands. The airmen's permanent unit, the 45th Fighter Squadron, had been sent to Baker Island, a small atoll north of the Gilberts from which the squadron bombed Tarawa from the other direction. Baker Island could sustain only half the squadron; the other half were the 400 airmen who were in my direct charge for several months until they were reunited with their squadron.

Seperated from their units as they were, they had no regular chain of command or supply channels. Further, having no set function, they were assigned the "dirty" details of the island, policing (cleaning up) of the areas of other groups and similar menial tasks. This was an unhappy situation that was exacerbated by the fact that a substantial number of the group assigned to me were non-commissioned officers who normally were spared such tasks. They were orphans and felt they were being treated as outcasts.

I have always believed in the potential of the human spirit when challenged, and at my prompting, in place of the policing details these men were assigned the most urgent, difficult and hazardous tasks, such as emergency loading of bombs on planes, by hand, which often required working through the night to get critical missions in the air. At the same time, I asked our group if they would agree to temporarily eliminate all rank, which they unanimously agreed to do (I offered to remove my insignia of rank but they rejected my offer).

The group developed a gung-ho spirit of determination and accomplishment, and, free from the encumbrance of rank, they approached each task no matter how difficult with an exhilarating sense of teamwork. The net result was that, though untrained in the specific functions, they broke all records for every task performed.

One of our least known but most satisfying achievements: We sent out forage units to beg and borrow every type of supply from other units on the island, pleading our orphan state. As a result, we were the best outfitted, best equipped and best fed soldiers in the Ellices-- and of most importance, we had a huge underground stockpile of the most precious item on the island--beer!

In the end, the work of our little group led to an air force commendation as the "inspiration" for the success of the entire mission.

Before that mission ended, a member of the General Staff of the Commanding General of the 7th Air Force, which was responsible for all air operations in the Central Pacific, flew down from Oahu to see me and requested that I fly back with him to take over the post of Intelligence Officer of Hickman Field, Oahu, the plush air base of the Air Corp. I agreed to do so but received permission to stay with my organization, the 3rd Assron, and return with them by ship several weeks later.

* * * *

I was fortunate in having interesting "jobs" throughout my three-year stay in the Pacific, including the period as Intelligence Officer of Hickman Field. One of my "ardous" extra duties at Hickman was responsibility for the Friday night fights! This earned me the undying appreciation of the Base Commander, who was a fight "nut," and led him to take me with him on an unwanted further mission "down under" as the Intelligence Officer of another expeditionary force!

Summary 2

American Naval Officer
accepts the surrender of
the mystery island Agui-
jan (3 to 4 miless off
Tinian). It was suppose
to be an empty island.?.
—*Courtesy of Jeff Weintraub*

(Left to Right) "Standby" a captured Japanese soldier, G2
Sam Weintraub, and "Toughie"

—*Courtesy of Jeff Weintraub*

G2 Sam Weintraub
locating Tinian Island.
—*Courtesy of Jeff Weintraub*
* Air Force G2 means security
officer

Sam Wintraub's view of Tinian Island, in the Marianas. (Big Picture- 1944;
insert picture- Today)

—*Courtesy of Jeff Wintraub*

Walter Phelan

—Courtesy of Steve Phelan

CHAPTER XIV
U.S. ARMY 106 INFANTRY DIVISION-
BATTLE OF THE BULGE

Journal by Walter J. Phelan

OCTOBER 21, 1944 THE DAY WE HAD BEEN WAITING
for dawned in a cool gray mist. With a degree of
apprehension and yes, some fear of the unknown, my
outfit, the 106th Infantry Division, embarked on the
British Ship Aquitania, the forth largest ship in the
world at that time, on a voyage that would take six
days from New York to the coast of Scotland.

We went by train to the Southwestern part of
England where we were billeted until the first week of
December. We crossed the English Channel from
Southampton and landed in France where we
bivouacked about one week. We spent one night in the
Black Forest among the largest snowflakes I had ever
seen. We knew we were getting ready to go on the line.
On December 8 Father Kelly, our chaplain, offered
Mass in honor of the Immaculate Conception of Mary.
It was raining so hard and the wind was blowing with
such force that the alter cards wouldn't stay in place
on the hood of the Jeep that Father Kelly used for an
altar. The old saying that there are "no atheists in
foxholes" came to mind as literally hundreds of troops
stayed for the entire Mass through the howling wind
and teeming rain.

We at this time were just two days from a trip across Belgium to our positions on the Siegfried Line. We relieved the Second Infantry Division and I remember an officer of the second telling our Company Commander that we were in a quiet sector and we probably wouldn't hear over one or two shots a day although German troops were only seven or eight hundred yards away from our outposts, which were about two hundred yards from our Company Command post or CP.

Our division had been activated at Fort Jackson, South Carolina in March, 1943. We took basic training in the summer of 1943. When I returned to Fort Jackson from a furlough to Memphis, Tennessee in late September I was astonished when I walked into my barracks and saw a great number of beds were turned back. Only then did I learn that while I was gone, approximately two weeks, about sixty men from my Company, (Company G), had been sent to a port of replacement. That figure represented almost a third of our Company strength, and every unit in the division gave up approximately the same percentage of men. Within a few weeks we started rebuilding our numbers with replacements and by the time we went on maneuvers in middle Tennessee in January, 1944, we were up to full strength.

In March, after eight weeks of maneuvers, we went to Camp Atterburg, Indiana. During the summer, we were raided again for replacements to be sent to Europe. Once more we lost almost a third of our troops and again we started getting replacements to bring our outfit up to required strength by the time we sailed to Europe in October. But even though we had the same number of men that we had in March, 1943, the esprit de corps was never the same. I have often wondered if we would have received the same casualties in the Battle of the Bulge if we had gone into battle with our original troops.

We were in place on the Siegfried Line from December 10 until December 17 when we withdrew after being attacked early in the morning of December 16. Of course we had no way of knowing that we were bearing the brunt of Germany's last offensive or breakthrough. They were attempting to split our supply lines and came perilously close to obtaining their objective.

Our division was spread very thinly apparently because G-2 or Army Intelligence did not think a major attack would occur there in the Ardennes Forest because of the treacherous terrain. But the enemy gathered several divisions and made an all out effort to destroy our forces. The fact we were spread so thinly and we were all so green contributed to our being completely surrounded in a few days. Our 422nd and 424th Regiment was in reserve. The 424th got out of the trap as a unit but it too suffered heavy losses. We bedded down on a high hill the night of December 18 and when we woke on the morning of the 19th, we were being shelled by 88 millimeter cannons. There was a higher hill about 300 yards away and we immediately descended the hill we were on and broke for the other one so that we would have the advantage of higher terrain. As we made our way across "no man's land" we were targets of the enemy's riflemen and the 88 millimeters behind their tanks. Our rifles were no match for their tanks.

We caught artillery fire the rest of December 19 and all morning of December 20. On the afternoon of December 20 a German officer and two runners under protection of a white flag made their way to our battalion headquarters and told the battalion executive officer that they knew we didn't have any artillery on our hill and that we knew what they had after approximately thirty hours of shelling. Our battalion commander had been wounded and had turned over his command to his executive officer. The German officer said that they would give us until 4 P.M. to accept their offer to capitulate. All of the officers of our battalion met and after much soul searching decided to accept their offer to prevent any additional loss of life. In looking back, I think that was probably a wise decision because even though we had higher ground that was the only advantage we had. We sent our messenger also under a white flag with our acceptance of their offer. We were instructed to walk down the hill the morning of December 21 with our hands behind us. We walked east for two days and were put into small box cars on December 23. That night after the cars had moved only a few miles the RAF (Royal Air Force) bombed the tracks and we were forced to stop. The next morning, December 24, after the fog lifted and after the tracks had been repaired the train was strafed by an American fighter plane. When the German guards opened the doors and let us out, we counted nine of our troops killed and forty-seven wounded. Our B-17's flew over in wave after wave.

The snow was ten to twelve inches deep and we stood in the open fields in human letters "U.S.A.P.O.W.". Several of our bombers tilted their wings to let us know they understood our situation. Several bombers were knocked out of the skies by anti-aircraft fire and we could count the number of parachutes from each plane shot down that opened. Whenever there were less than ten we knew that some of the airmen didn't get out because of B-17 bombers had a crew of 10.

We were herded back into the cars that night and the next day, Christmas, we were let out of the cars and given a piece of bread with something like molasses. We were told that we would be in Mayen the next night after a two day march at which time we would then get some more food.

We reached Mayen on schedule but there was no food nor was there any the next day or the following day until that night when we were given another piece of bread and a small amount of cheese. That meant that from the date of our capture, December 21, until December 28 we had two pieces of bread plus a little bit of molasses and the small ration of cheese. We walked another two days and were put in box cars again for the last day's journey to Camp 4-B, about eighty kilometers or fifty miles from Dresden. In the ten days we walked about 150 miles.

After three weeks, one hundred of us were sent on a working commando to a town called Roitch. Then, after two more weeks we were put on a train and sent to Merseberg where we were housed in an old beer hall for about two and half months. Our routine was to go out every morning and dig out drainage ditches or filling in bomb craters. We decided to strike one day and then get a bowl of watery soup and a bread ration when we returned to the lager in late afternoon. They said they would remedy that by giving us our bread and soup in the morning. The soup usually had a few pieces of potato just a barely a piece or two of meat.

On April 13, we could hear artillery fire and were put on the road for another march of about 125 miles to a big wooded area near the Elba River. We built lean-tos from pine branches to shield ourselves from the elements.

On April 24, we started walking west and at about noon, we entered the town of Wurzen, Germany, where I saw an M-P from the 69th Infantry Division directing traffic. The first thing we asked him was, "Where is the chow truck?"

I ate so many peanut butter and jelly sandwiches that I got sick. What may have played a part in my getting sick were the onion and raw egg that I found in a barn before we got to Wurzen.

We were trucked to a staging area from where we were sent to a Recovered Allied Military Personnel (RAMP) camp in France where we were placed on a soft bland diet for the first few days and gradually were given more highly seasoned food. I weighed about 110 pounds when I was liberated but by the time I arrived at Fort Dix, New Jersey on June 12 I was up to 157 pounds.

Remagen Bridgehead
—*Courtesy of The Lightning: The History of the 78th Infantry Division*

Carolyn and
Walter Phelan
—*Courtesy of Steve Phelan*

CHAPTER XV
THE MARSHALL ISLANDS
/ THE MARIANAS

Story of Tony Muscarella

The Marshall Islands:

TONY MUSCARELLA WAS FROM TRUCKEE, CALIFORNIA near Lake Tahoe. His "war skills" came from hunting with his father as a youth and he had great night vision. Tony said that there was a General they called "Howling Mad" Smith who was in charge of all the Marines. Colonel Cates was in charge of Tony's 4th Marine Division.

E Company of the 4th Marine Division was Tony's outfit. Tony was an expert machine gunner. Their divisions' target was Roi Namur Island, a part of the Kwajalein Atoll in the Center part of the Marshall Islands. There were 20,000 Japanese troops on the larger centrally located Kwajalein Atoll and its adjoining islands. The Roi Namur Island had an even smaller speck of island land next to it that could be wadded to at low tide. The Japanese had a working radio base there. Tony's E Company's objective was to take that radio base. Tony told me this took only forty minutes to secure the tiny speck of an island.

The 4th Marine Division had 19,000 "young heroes" committed to taking The Marshall Islands. Tony said the Navy blew up the fuel dump on Roi Namur Island and it shook the whole island. Tony said he witnessed pill boxes destroyed by flame-throwing Marine tanks. The tanks saved many Marine lives. The fuel dump on Roi Namur Island filled up with sea water and became a lake in a day or two. Roi Namur Island was elevated only two feet tall above the Coral and Pacific Ocean. It was geographically much like New Orleans; the native people there buried their dead above ground in crypts. Tony said he saw a Japanese Betty Bomber partially destroyed on the ground at Roi Namur Island. The astonished 4th Marine Division found Delmonté canned goods there that had been stolen from the Philippians warehouses in 1942.

The 4th Marine Division liberated two American nurses who were captured at the Fall of Corregidor at Manila. Unfortunately, they were drugged and used as prostitutes. The US Government never made this known to the public. The 4th Marine Division was very upset with the treatment of American P.O.W.'s by the Japanese. The nurses were sent to an asylum in the USA. Tony told me that the Japanese had practically destroyed their minds.

Saipan- in the Marianas:

Saipan was in the Mariana Island chain and had many coffee plantations, lots of banana groves, and an abundance of palm trees. It was very green and plush and also had a beautiful Japanese prayer place. 30,000 Japanese were on Saipan including the "Red Collar Division" who were responsible for the Nanking China Civilian Atrocities. There they killed innocent men, women, and children. The Japanese also had an Imperial Marine Regiment stationed there. They are always taller in stature and fiercer fighters than regular Japanese Army troops.

On June 15, 1944 the 2nd and 4th Marine Divisions invaded Saipan. Tony said the battleship TN lobbed enormous shells at the Japanese and devastated their defenses. The defensive firepower from Japanese mortars and rifle sniper fire was very heavy. Of the 29,000 Japanese on Saipan only 1,000 surrendered and were captured.

Tony's battle buddies were Dan Douglas and Vannucci. Tony was wounded coming down from Mount Tapochau. A Marine tanker pulled him up inside his tank to give Tony a chance for survival. The tanker's name was Mr. Boatwright who was an Assistant Fire Chief from Memphis, TN. Tony was taken from Saipan to Guam to get patched up.

Today, Saipan has a very well kept American cemetery. Tony Muscarella wrote a story of his experiences on Iwo Jima in his book *The Young Heroes*. He received two Purple Hearts, two Presidential citations, and The Silver Star. He is missed but his brave spirit still lives among Americans who knew him or read his heroic oral history as told in his book, *The Young Heroes*. May God always keep his spirit with us.

Tony Muscarella
—Courtesy of Dino's Restaurant

GI's at the Rainbow Corner Red Cross Club in Paris, France, whoop it up after buying the special edition of the Paris Post, which carried the banner headline, "JAPS QUIT". – August 10, 1945

—*Courtesy of National Archives*

Japan's Surrender

—*Courtesy of National Archives*

Japanese soldiers saluting the American Flag. - 1945

—*Courtesy of National Archives*

Richard Heim (front row, 1ˢᵗ on left)

—*Courtesy of Rose Heim*

CHAPTER XVI
SHOT DOWN OVER YUGOSLAVIA

Oral Journal of Richard Heim

IT WAS 1943 WHEN I JOINED THE CREW OF B24 Yellow F. My first crew had crashed in training and with it the life of the flight engineer, when the upper gun turret collapsed on his legs. Five members of that crew were hurt and I was miraculously spared. I had loaned the pilot my altitude equipment and proceeded to go back to the barracks. It was then that I was transferred to the crew of Yellow F. We had been trained at Chatham Field, Georgia. From there our journey brought us to New York's Mitchell Field. There we were allowed to pick up Yellow F for our voyage to Gander, New Foundland by way of Bangor, Maine. Then, we flew across the Atlantic to the Azores Islands. Our sojourn pointed us onto North Africa and then we finally arrived in Southern Italy. Our base was in the approximate area of *Foggia* and *Canosa di Puglia*. The U.S. Fifteenth Army Air Force was our ultimate destination.

Our crew was a good mixture of what America is all about. Our pilot, Lieutenant Scottie Stewart was from Pratt and Whitney Stock. His dad was one of the top officers from that company. Our Sperry Ball under turret operator was Powell Robinson, a very preppy son of a New Jersey Banker.

I was our tail gunner, just barely 18 years of age. I had to finish my college education some 4 to 5 years later. I had just entered Penn State when World War II interrupted my college training. It wasn't hard to enlist in the Army Air Force. George Chiozza our nose gunner was the son of an Italian immigrant family. He was soon to be known as "*The Echo*" and I, Staff Sergeant Richard Heim, was called "*The Shadow*". He being the nose gunner and myself being the tail gunner of the ship we were ultimately to fly in combat.

Our radio operator was Claude Martin from Arkansas, "Arkie Razorback" and he also was a gunner. Our assistant radio operator was Joe Sidlack proud owner of some 250 acres of wheat fields in Enid, Oklahoma.

We had all flown several missions in training and upon our arrival, to what was the ultimate destination; we had many experiences reminiscent of the episodes of M.A.S.H. I can still remember the time back at Fifteenth Army Air Force base when someone had the bright idea in the sea of mud to put heating units inside our tents. People proceeded to the flight line to take the discarded fuel tanks from P-51's as a reservoir and inverted oil drums into a cement area with a u-tube heating the very combustible mixture. As I expected much to the chagrin of the unit, tent after tent began to pop and blow up throughout the staging area.

On an earlier Greek mission our substitute ship which had never been named had the reputation as one of the finest B-24's in our squadron. It had an impeccable safety record and was judged mechanically perfect. It was supposed to be called "Salonica Sal", in reference to a previous mission where it was one of two B24's that returned from Greece partially intact.

On that Greek mission our Sperry ball gunner; Powell Robinson received flack under his seat which broke our hydraulic fuel lines. In shock, he thought he was hit but the red fluid on his flight uniform proved to be nothing more than hydraulic fluid and we laughed nervously as we returned to base.

Our crew was very close. Personally we had completed a great number of combat missions together before November 17, 1944, the day we were shot down. On that mission we were to fly to and bomb Black Hammer South. This German target was a *synthetic oil refinery* some 90 miles South East of Berlin. This was usually a "piece of cake" or "milk run" as it was done during daytime by precision bombing. We dispersed into the skies aluminum sheets to throw the German radar installations off track. But somehow on that fateful day, we were caught in an unsuspected short burst of 88mm anti-aircraft fire. It ruptured our main fuel tank. Then we just sailed along for a while, dropping our high octane fuel, just trying to limp back to the base.

On this fateful November 17, 1944 mission, it was not even our own ship for we had transferred Yellow F to another crew so they could finish their 25 missions in relative safety.

We had loaned part of our crew; our co-pilot and

navigator to the second crew to fly our Yellow F. We then assumed control of the B24, a.k.a. "Dottie D" on this mission. "Dottie D" was due to be named Dottie the Whore but the group air commander took the word "whore" off and left it as "Dottie D". Then we heard the name was going to be changed to "Dottie the New Hampshire Troubadour".

As we limped home in "Dottie D", Yellow F was on our wing, we saw her very distinctly. Our navigator and co-pilot were flying beside us as we discharged gasoline and we gave them the sign we are soon to bail out: - "out of fuel over Yugoslavia".

The bail out button rang as Powell Robinson, our Sperry ball gunner was excreting in the urinal and we all made the rush to our respective bail out hatches. I was the second to last to leave the plane. As our chutes opened, I could see the echo - George Chiozza some thousand yards away singing my then favorite song "That Old Black Magic" and nervously shouting from 10,000 feet "Down and down we go - round and round we go."

And as I lost sight of those parachutes, I hit the top of a Shellrock Peak sliding down and injuring my cheek and leg. We had $48 worth of escape kit money on that mission and a U.S. Colt 45 revolver. I hid behind a boulder and I could see what was a group of rag tag soldiers proceeding up the mountain shouting "Partizono, Partizono". As I peeked from behind that rock I then realized *I was in safe hands.*

I soon joined Claude Martin (Arkie-Razorback) who was on the floor of a peasant's shack having consumed a large quantity of Arak (high proof Licorice

Spirit). He was feeling no pain with a large crab apple in one hand and the clear liquid spirit in the other. We proceeded from there, trying to collect each member of our crew but realized several were missing. The co-pilot flying with us had landed in Chetniks lands in Yugoslavia. There was a Civil war, the German sympathizers were Chetniks and we had allied ourselves with the Partisans. The pilot was nowhere in sight. He finally appeared having been carried down from the mountaintop from the vicinity of Janine. A pitched battle had raged on either side of him between the Chetniks and Partisans. His leg was broken in several places but Joe Sidlack (Oklahoma) having Czech ancestry, conversed with the Partisan aides and soon assisted in communicating his pain. He explained the troublesome spots and helped the doctor to set his leg.

We then proceeded to Drvar, Yugoslavia. Drvar was the headquarters of Tito's army at one time. His headquarters was actually behind a waterfall cascading magnificently down a shell rock mountain precipice. We viewed destroyed Axis gliders everywhere from an ill fated Italian Glider Brigade. Our American planes flew over regularly on missions to Germany. We saw them at very high altitude passing over from time to time. We were ushered into a bombed out compound where we were to sleep and pass our stay in this mountain strong hold. Partisans were everywhere. Women wore hand grenades around their waist. This was a life and death struggle for all in war time!

Soon we were asleep under our silken parachutes exhausted from our journey and knowing full well it would be a while before we reached home again.

One of the unusual traits of our stay in Drvar was the food we ate. We had soup without messa, (soup without meat). We always wondered where those beautiful portions of lamb ended. We were soon to find out having been invited to the commandant's house, where we saw the commandant eating with all the splendor of a beautifully prepared private chef dinner. So, Tito's Communist society was quite capitalistic after all.

Many days passed in Drvar and we continued to pick up many allied air people who jumped in the surrounding countryside. We had no place to go but onward to our next destination. We did so by going up the mountains and through the mountain passes in a wood burning locomotive attached to several boxcars. It was cold, freezing below 0 temperatures and if our hands were wet for any reason whatsoever any contact with the metal of the boxcar would soon remove a piece of our skin from our fingers. As we chugged along through the mountains we knew that we never would forget the little quaint train. We then reached what was to be our final destination before our trip home. It was located near Sanskimost; the cross road city of that Yugoslavian area with many ethnic denominations. We viewed Moslems calling from Minarets at every half hour of the day, a Tradition Sarde in a monotone voice. We viewed that wondrous Catholic Church that had been bombed out and ruined. There, inside we passed many days going to service with Catholic members of our crew. We viewed many Russian and Orthodox religion partisans scurrying about. We had relatively better housing.

One day in Sanskimost, Powell Robinson was cleaning his gun. We were biding our time playing with our newly constructed football game. It was ferreted out of bits of wood which we made into dice. We had a whole series of instructions for our board football game. As we lay under the bombed out ruins, Powell's gun accidentally discharged over our heads and the bullet lodged into a ceramic light socket without a switch. Naturally, we were frightened; Powell almost discharged a second shot before we knocked the gun from his hand by reflex action. The partisans scurried in from everywhere, surveying the scene and looked at the light switch. Their response and chant was unanimous: "Dobro Americano, Dobro Americano" — "Good Shot, Good Shot". They thought Powell was aiming at the light switch for target practice.

Two foreign missions were assigned to the town, one a young British mission, the other a Russian mission. Both kept tabs on our activities. We use to pass the time arguing whether the Ljubuska - Yugoslavia cigarettes were fatter in circumference than our American version. Food drops came by parachute and we were very grateful for such items as bitter British Marmalade and cooked small provisions. Our ranks swelled from other Americans gathered from the countryside and local inflation occurred just by the $48 converted to Dinar from each American's escape kit. We were put in protective custody for our own safekeeping and even though we had the run of the countryside we were tacitly assigned a guard to watch our comings and goings.

It was then that I contacted the dreadful flea bites which became infected and I was sent to the Partisan hospital where they were short of bandages and performed operations without anesthesia. One such operation was performed on the appendix of a young partisan soldier who occupied the bed opposite me. Because of excruciating pain he almost swallowed his tongue. The conditions in the hospital were very primitive; bandages were washed and rewashed, used and reused over and over again. Gangrened legs which had been amputated were piled up in the hallways. God bless those brave Partisan freedom fighters, both men and women who saved our lives from Nazi capture or death.

We stayed in Sanskimost for some time. About that time our co-pilot was smuggled through the Chetniks into Allied hands, he first traveled with the Germans as a Chetnik and was then transported to Split, Yugoslavia and finally to Italy to fly again. He and Michael Aros were subsequently killed in action. We continued to reside in Yugoslavia waiting for a break to take us home. That break occurred in Mid-January 1945. The delay was excruciating because every available aircraft had been assigned to the Battle of the Bulge. The Balkin air force would not dare risk coming to rescue us. Finally, a snow covered plowed field with carbide lights was set up for this purpose. What a welcome sight to see those Dakotas coming through with Spitfire escort and land on that bumpy runway.

Subsequently, we returned to Bari, Italy and after an intelligence debriefing, we were shipped home by way of Bermuda and then to Miami where I called my folks. My folks had not yet received the message from the War Department that I was safe from missing in action. Ironically enough as the celebration began at my house after my return home; I received a message from the War Department that I was safe from missing in action.

This was the most unusual experience of my combat life and will keep the memories with me always. I was blessed recently by having a reunion with my crew in Nashville, TN.

Richard Heim passed away recently. He was a dauntless "true rock patriot". May his spirit stay with all Americans.

Richard Heim
—*Courtesy of Rose Heim*

In a prisoner-of-war inclosure a look of defiance is found among more complacent
expressions.

—*Courtesy of The Lightning: The History of the 78th Infantry Division*

CHAPTER XVII
THE UPSIDE DOWN B 29

Story of Chester Marshall

CHESTER MARSHALL IS THE AUTHOR OF SIX BOOKS. Chester grew up in Belzoni, MS. I interviewed him and got this short oral history from Chester.

Chester has said that the B 29 was made primarily by women at Boeing. I recommend his books *Sky Giants over Japan : The Global Twentieth Century.* Chester told me the story about the B 29-Bataan Avenger being turned upside down by a huge firestorm and wind shears over Japan. The Bataan Avenger weighed between 120,000 and 140,000 pounds, depending on the bomb loads. Very strong wind shears from the fires in a Japanese city flipped her over. Her lights went out and the pilot searched for his flashlight to read his instruments. They told him that she was upside down. He finally regained control of her and returned to Saipan.

Chester was a member of The Twentieth Air Force, 73 Wing, 499 Bomb Group, and 878th Squadron. Do not be confused- A Wing has four groups. Three squadrons make up a group. Thus, you have twelve total squadrons per group.

Saipan, was captured by the 4th Marine Division on July 1,1944. It is only 1,500 miles from Japan. Chester would have to fly a twelve to fifteen hour mission. After Iwo Jima fell, a fighter escort was available as Chester flew near the tiny island.

Chester usually flew eight missions in sixteen days. His crew would have a one hour briefing the night before. Chester would get up at 3 a.m., and he had to be on the line with the other B 29's at 5 a.m. His take off time was 6 a.m. Chester would be bombing Japan around 12 o'clock noon. Chester would return to Saipan between 6 p.m. and   8 p.m. depending on wind and weather. Upon landing on Saipan, he would have a one to two hour debriefing by an Army Air Force interrogator. On one mission they had to ditch four of his squadron's planes, which had been damaged over Japan.

Chester's B 29, Mary Ann, did thirty combat missions. Bob Morgan of Memphis Belle fame flew in the 29th Air Force. He piloted a B29 called the Dauntless Dottie.

A crippled B 29 flown by Chester Marshall landed March 16, 1945 on Iwo Jima's fighter plane airfield. It was a very short runway. The marines said it was secure but some holdouts came out at night and killed army troops in their barracks while they were asleep. Chester had an uneasy feeling that night on Iwo Jima and did not sleep a wink.

Chester and Lois Marshall

—Courtesy of Edwin Frank

Paul Vescovo

—Courtesy of Paul and Shirley Vescovo

CHAPTER XVIII
THE B24 - UMBRIAGO OVER HUNGARY

Story of Paul Vescovo

PAUL VESCOVO IS ONE OF THE BRAVEST WWII AIRMEN that I have ever interviewed. He and a friend saved the life of a sick Chicago Airman by literally carrying him through a death march that lasted for over 90 Days. This is his personal WWII Oral Autobiography that follows.

They took off at dawn in their B24 called "Umbriago". Their plane was named after a famous song by Jimmy Durante. The date was July 7, 1944. Their target was Breslau, Germany, the longest mission that they ever flew. This was the biggest oil refinery in Europe. On the way back, he was shot down 70 miles southwest of Budapest, Hungary. Hungary had sided with and joined the axis military forces. Their Army joined the German Army to fight the Russian Army on the Eastern Front. Paul's plane experienced heavy anti-aircraft flack during their initial bomb run. Two of Umbriago's four engines were knocked out. Umbriago lost altitude and could not stay in tight formation. They became prey for two German fighters, a ME 109 and a Focke-Wulf 190. The plane caught fire and they bailed out before the plane blew up. This was his 31st combat mission. Paul was the last man to bail out. He was the radio operator and the waist gunner for B24-Umbriago. The nose gunner mistakenly had placed his parachute on backwards and couldn't bail out! Suddenly the ME 109 hit the plane's fuel tank with a 20mm cannon burst. That fuel tank explosion blew the nose gunner out and saved his life. He pulled the rip cord and landed safely. Only Paul and four others made it out. Unfortunately, five other fellow Airmen perished in the explosion.

Paul landed in a wheat field where two Hungarians captured him. They tried to beat him with wooden sticks and axe handles but Paul was very strong and took the sticks and axe handles from the brutal Hungarians. He was held in a civilian prison for about 60 days. In prison he was only fed soapy, weak-tasting soup. Then he was put on a train for his P.O.W. camp Stalag Luft 4 near Gdansk, Poland. This was Paul's last train ride before his liberation. Stalag Luft 4 was on the Baltic Sea and especially cold. The prison guards heard the Russians were coming so a death march started February 8, 1945. Paul was unfortunately forced by his beastly prison guards to walk for 90 days. They started at dawn and ended at dusk. Paul and his fellow P.O.W.'s were forced to sleep in fields with no change of clothes. They suffered from lice, ticks, and other vermin through the rain, wind, and sleet during one of the coldest winters Europe had ever experienced. It had brutally affected Paul and his fellow P.O.W.'s. If you fell down or slowed down the German guards would shoot you or let their dogs kill you. Paul and a fellow airman carried a sick Chicagoan between their shoulders for 90 days of walking through Hell.

On May 8, 1945, they had reached the town of Follingbostel, Germany between Hanover and Hamburg. The German guards had fled a few days earlier with their beastly dogs. They were liberated by Field Marshall Montgomery's 7th Armor. They were given cafeteria food and they ate too much, because their stomachs had shrunk. Unfortunately this made them quite ill because they had not been used to eating *normal* portions of food. They could not keep the food down, and they went around the corner of the barracks and vomited. Finally, they were sent to a POW rehab unit in London, England where they were nurtured back to health.

Before the death march, Paul weighed in at a healthy 175 pounds and in those 11 months while he was captured, he lost 40 pounds! It took several years for his stomach to get back to normal.

These facts about the death march were never brought to the American public's attention. I hope that Paul's story of bravery and determination will continue to be told to all future American generations.

gJk/rbp

WAR DEPARTMENT

THE ADJUTANT GENERAL'S OFFICE

IN REPLY REFER TO:
AG 201 Vescovo, Paul J.
PC-N NAT165

WASHINGTON 25, D. C.

24 July 1944

Mrs. Ida Vescovo
584 South Cox Street
Memphis, Tennessee

Dear Mrs. Vescovo:

This letter is to confirm my recent telegram in which you were regretfully informed that your son, Technical Sergeant Paul J. Vescovo, 34,508,620, Air Corps, has been reported missing in action over Germany since 7 July 1944.

I know that added distress is caused by failure to receive more information or details. Therefore, I wish to assure you that at any time additional information is received it will be transmitted to you without delay, and, if in the meantime no additional information is received, I will again communicate with you at the expiration of three months. Also, it is the policy of the Commanding General of the Army Air Forces upon receipt of the "Missing Air Crew Report" to convey to you any details that might be contained in that report.

The term "missing in action" is used only to indicate that the whereabouts or status of an individual is not immediately known. It is not intended to convey the impression that the case is closed. I wish to emphasize that every effort is exerted continuously to clear up the status of our personnel. Under war conditions this is a difficult task as you must readily realize. Experience has shown that many persons reported missing in action are subsequently reported as prisoners of war, but as this information is furnished by countries with which we are at war, the War Department is helpless to expedite such reports. However, in order to relieve financial worry, Congress has enacted legislation which continues in force the pay, allowances and allotments to dependents of personnel being carried in a missing status.

Permit me to extend to you my heartfelt sympathy during this period of uncertainty.

Sincerely yours,

J. A. ULIO
Major General,
The Adjutant General.

Paul Vescovo's Missing In Action letter (MIA)

—Courtesy of Paul and Shirley Vescovo

Paul Vescovo and
James Edwards(first
black actor)
—*Courtesy of Paul and
Shirley Vescovo*

B24- Umbriago
—*Courtesy of Paul Vescovo*

Released POWs—
Augst 1945
—*Courtesy of National Archives*

Shirley and Paul
Vescovo
—*Courtesy of Paul and
Shirley Vescovo*

Buddy Bradfield

—Courtesy of Jerry Bradfield

CHAPTER XIX
PLATOON STORIES

Story of Buddy Bradfield

Easter Breakfast

AS WE SAT AROUND THE "PORTABLE FIELD MESS FACILITY", my platoon looked very professional. Patton's Third Army had been a great training force for all of us. We had been through Normandy, The Battle of the Bulge and the crossing of the Rhein River.

I had won two bronze crosses for valor and still didn't want to be promoted to Second Lieutenant. The "Life Span" of a Second Lieutenant in the Third Army was indeed short. I knew this from watching them break from cover to lead us and then their being mowed down by the Germans.

As we ate Easter breakfast, the Germans lobbed metal armor piercing shells into our camp. We continued to eat since the shells didn't explode but only made a thud as they hit the ground. They must be completely out of ammunition, we thought. Then suddenly… it began, "a full scale mortar attack". We were abruptly up on our feet and jogged onto a nearby autobahn away from the inconvenience. Afterwards, our Colonel, was very upset about our Easter Breakfast Sojourn. He said, "not only did you run, Easter Eggs and all, but you also left all of your equipment in the camp. The Germans could have come on in and helped themselves."

Eleven Men in a Cellar

The normal size of a platoon is 56 soldiers. Some members of my platoon "liked wine a little too much". We had just liberated the hillside town of Ribeauville in Alsace. Our tanks hadn't even stopped to check the town out for Germans. Eleven of my platoon left us and decided to celebrate deep down in a wine cellar west of town. The Germans just threw a concussion grenade into it and knocked our men unconcouscious. They were then immediately picked up by a German truck and taken to a P.O.W. Camp. The next few days, the rest of my platoon and the rest of the Third Army Obtained from the "tasting" of any wines!

American armor rumbles down to a treadway for the Roer River crossing as infantrymen await orders to cross.

—Courtesy of Lightning: The History of the 78th Infantry Division

Alert! A Browning automatic rifle and a caliber .30 light machine gun manned by two infantrymen.

—*Courtesy of The Lightning: The History of the 78th Infantry Division*

A first sergeant directs a tank in mopping up and clearing battle-scarred Euskirchen, railroad hub of the Cologne Plain
—*Courtesy of The Lightning: The History of the 78th Infantry Division*

Jean and Buddy Bradfield

—*Courtesy of Jerry Bradfield*

Simon "Spider" Webb

—*Courtesy of Spider Webb*

CHAPTER XX
THE PARADE

Journal by Simon "Spider" Webb

Simon "Spider" Webb

"My God," Bob exclaimed. "I was a junior at Rhode Island when these guys left home!" "Hell," I thought to myself, "we've only been marines two-and-a-half years, and they've been gone four." It was about 9:30 a.m. January 8, 1944 in Sydney, Australia as we watched The Australian Eighth Brigade return home parade.

Robert W. "Bob" Marshall and I met when he joined Marine Scout Bombing Squadron - 243 in July 1942. We became friends quickly, we were squadron mates for two years, and shared many R&Rs, breathtaking adventures, and later happy reunions before he died in 1995. Bob was from Pawtucket, Rhode Island and I from Helena, Arkansas, same age and height, bachelors, loved to fly and teamed on liberty and R&R. In those first years we flew a lot, partied a lot, and hopefully matured a bit while progressing to wingman 2nd Lieutenants to division leader Captains. We bonded as only combat comrades and drinking buddies do. Overseas we bunked in four-man tents with Jim "Jimbo" Grubbs from Minot, ND and Joe "Jose" Shelton from Abilene, TX.

In Sydney, Australia we accidentally experienced one of the most memorable happy shared events in our long friendship. We members of 243 flight echelon had been rotated by air from Munda Point, New Georgia in the Soloman Islands on January 2nd to our rear base on Efate in the New Hebrides.

For six weeks we had provided close air-ground support, offshore ship-fire spotting, and bombed Japanese forces elsewhere during the Third Marine Division's landing on Bougainville. On January 6th we were flown in bucket-seat R4Ds (DC3) to Tontouta, New Caledonia to spend the night, open-bed trucked to Noumea, then transported to Sydney in an unheated, uncomfortable and noisy Navy PBM flying boat for a one week R&R.

After the inevitable paperwork and delays checking into The Prince of Wales Hotel, operated for transient American officers, a taxi to the two legendary pubs in The Hotel Australia was Priority One. It was summer down under and great to again be in liberty khakis with field scarves, shined shoes and a place to spend money. After three months of no liquor ration or fresh foods, we were more than ready for adult beverages - and the fleshpots of civilization. We had earned it, and were damned well going to enjoy it.

The corner street-level pub was stand-up and male only with pretty barmaids accustomed to thirsty American servicemen. We were quickly introduced to warm beer poured from pitchers - delicious, refreshing and, best of all plentiful. They knew American soldiers stationed in Sydney had not been in combat and called them King's Cross

Commandoes. American Marines with their oblong eyes, Atabrine tans, dry palates, happy banter, and tales of do-and-daring were obviously on R&R, had lots of money, and tipped well -- just typical red-blooded American boys living every day a holiday and every night Saturday night. We happily struggled back to our room and collapsed.

Come morning with predictable dry mouths and throbbing headaches and no hair-of-the-dog-that-bit-us, we faced a dilemma for pubs didn't open until ten. A bit out of practice in dealing with hangovers, I took a shower followed by "stike & iggs" in the hotel dining room to fortify us till opening time. There was much banter among our friends, other marines and Navy types during the meal. A table of Air Corps types in a corner, resplendent in their pinks with floppy visored caps on the table seemed embarrassed to have to share space with uncouth Marines. None of us wore campaign or personal decoration ribbons while they had American and Pacific Theatre ribbons only. Probably trash-hauling transport jocks, so we ignored them.

About nine we caught a bus into downtown and started walking toward the Hotel Australia, enjoying the fresh city street lights, sounds and smells, and watching real live women walk around. The only females we had seen at Munda were three French nuns in black gowns and wide white wimples herding native Melanesian pygmies onto a plane for evacuation. If there were any Navy nurses, we didn't see them, probably because many sick or injured were airlifted to Guadalcanal for treatment. Also, neither the USO nor Red Cross had ventured that far forward.

At the Hotel Australia street crossing Bob said, "What's that beat I hear?" For the first time I became aware of a distant drumbeat and together we looked and listened, watching other pedestrians, to faint sounds of music. Plenty of time before opening, so we followed the crowd another block where the street was lined with spectators looking toward the increasing volume of martial music and crowd roar.

I asked an older man what was happening, and he replied, "It's the Eyeth Brigeyed home after four years." We were astounded. Four years away to the war. Our backs straightened up for these blokes had suffered more than their share. We were thinking twelve months from the States was tough duty.

Ah, the shifting sights, sounds and electricity in the air as the colors approached followed by a band, and the proud veterans of the Eighth. No shiny leather or brightly burnished buttons here. Weather-beaten faces and arms, short sleeve khaki shirts and shorts, knee high stockings and hob-nailed boots, left hat brim pinned up, rifles flat on shoulders and left arms swinging in the exaggerated English style. They exuded confidence and pride. I later commented, "They were right out of Hollywood Central Casting."

Marching along within and outside of their ranks were hundreds of happy women and children, obviously family, holding onto their rifle arms and/ or touching them in any fashion. Many carried flags and others open bottles. The crowd roar became deafening. Bob and I proudly joined the many uniformed bystanders by popping to and saluting as their colors passed. By then I was starry-eyed and thirsty as hell! In the bar we heard the full story.

The Australian Army Eighth Brigade left home for Egypt in 1939, before Hitler started WWII by invading Poland. They went to Greece to help stem that German advance only to be pushed out to Crete. The Germans forced them from there into North Africa. They were bypassed at Tobruk, Libya when the Germans pushed Montgomery's British Army into Egypt, and became part of the beleaguered forces the press dubbed The Tobruk Rats. When freed by the British advance west, they were sent home to regroup and retrain. While enroute the Japanese advanced down the Malay Peninsula toward Singapore where they disembarked to join its defenses. All of Singapore's defenses were seaward leaving the landside undefendable, so the Eighth reembarked for Australia.

En route they were hurriedly put ashore at Port Moresby, New Guinea to help defend against a threatening Japanese force. This time General MacArthur's island-hopping campaign cut off the Japanese and relived Port Moresby. Those we saw in parade were the survivors of that too-little-and-too-late four-year trek. They were true heroes.

We met and chatted with a sergeant downing a few before catching a train to his home in the outback, and kept his glass full as the story of their travels unfolded intermingled with personal experiences, which included bearing body parts to show scars. A totally different war from ours, and a humbling experience.

Later Bob and I discovered we had similar thought patterns at the time. Would the folks back in Pawtucket/Helena welcome us home the same way? Of course we had to get back first, the odds of which neither of us really wanted to dwell upon at the time. Bottom line: neither ever participated in a homecoming parade or celebration.

Seeing the wildly supportive crowd and meeting veterans of the Australia Eighth Brigade put the war in a different perspective. They suffered many casualties and had been continually engaged for four years, always getting the short end of the stick. I often mused about their future. I doubt they saw more action, and were released after the war and sent home as were my friends and I.

Whenever I see stories of or read stories about the Australian outback I cannot help but wonder if anyone I saw that day may have been involved.

Many years later my son Tom called from Sydney to verify the hotel name, for I had asked that he, if ever there, hoist one for me. The hotel had been razed for an office building many years before so he happily hoisted one for old dad in another pub.

In my mind's eye the Eyeth Brigeyed is still proudly parading before an enthusiastic crowd, the barmaids are happily pouring yet another for us thirsty Yanks, and I can again lose the bonds of earth and soar with the eagles.

Semper Fi!

Simon L. "Spider" Webb, DFC

Naval Aviator

LtCol USMCR

May 2006

"Spider" is on the second row from the bottom, 3rd from the right.

—*Courtesy of Spider Webb*

Simon "Spider" Webb
—*Courtesy of Spider Webb*

CHAPTER XXI
THE RANCH

Journal by Simon "Spider" Webb

A cattle ranch on Hawaii? Yes, and it clashed with the poplar concept this Arkansas boy had of hula dancers swaying to ukulele music on a sunny, sandy beach beneath rustling palm trees, and a pounding surf.

Many years ago a man named Parker established what was to become a thriving cattle ranch on the largely barren high plateau between the twin peaks, Mauna Loa and Mauna Kea, on the *Big Island* of Hawaii, Territory of Hawaii. Few, other than islanders, knew of its existence- and could care less, for it was all but inaccessible.

Years, decades, generations, hurricanes, and lava flows came and went, bringing better roads, transportation and modern conveniences like electricity, radios, and telephones. Yet the Parker Ranch remained largely unknown at the tail end of a *No Outlet* road. In 1943 the United States Army built a base there.

Marine Scout Bombing Squadron 243, fresh from the States, arrived at Ewa Marine Corps Air Station on Oahu in January 1943, and was divided between Johnston and Palmyra Islands on The Hawaiian Sea Frontier from March to September.

Ours was a largely boring tour of duty with no enemies disrupting our routines; our harm's way the built-in risks of flying single-engine aircraft over a vast and lonely Pacific.

George Wolverton, Jim Grubbs and I were on Johnston while my friend Bob Marshall was at Palmyra. George, an army brat, knew a lot about the Hawaiian Islands, having graduated from high school in Honolulu. During the months on Johnston he told many tales about his growing-up years and sights in the islands.

When the squadron reunited at Ewa, untempered in combat, the aircrew members were given a week R&R. Jim and I were curious about the Big Island and George agreed to show us around. Commercial air to Hilo, in a rented 1940 stick-shift black Ford 4-door sedan, lots of cash, and two six-packs, we were on our way; intending to drive the perimeter of the island in three days and two nights.

The road north of Hilo ran through canopies of large forested areas inhabited by a variety of birds and strange sweet smelling blossomed bushes, and openings with the blue expanse of the Pacific on our right. There were many signs of civilization but not the *little grass shacks* of Hollywood. We passed through small villages with unpronounceable names like Papa'ikou, Papeeko' Hakalau, Papa'aloa, Laupahoehoe and Pa'auilo. George explained that all vowels are pronounced. All had chickens, goats and mostly modern dress. We stopped at wooded and flower strewn scenic spots like Wailoa River, Rainbow Falls, and Alaska Falls. It was all strange and marvelous to us North Dakota and Arkansas boys. The beer was delicious, and I never did find out how Alaska got to Hawaii.

At a pits stop and beer resupply, George asked about possible accommodations for the night. Among them was an army camp up on *the ranch.* Sounded like an O-Club, mess hall, and economical transients quarters to us. We got directions and went. Leaving the shore and its foliage we followed an upland winding road inland to the almost treeless inland plateau with an ocean horizon in most directions. Then came the surprise.

The sign at the gate said UNITED STATES ARMY HOSPITAL. Visible were many large and small tents, with little human activity. With instructions at the gate, we found the Officer of the Day and were assigned a pyramidal tent with four cots. Another surprise was that the installation was brand new with no patients beyond their own personnel. Built to treat and support future causalities; it was over ready. The fun began in the O-Club.

Three hale, hearty, deeply tanned, and thirsty, single Marine Corps captain naval aviators became the center of attraction when we entered. The place was full of doctors, nurses and other medical types already bored with isolation and inactivity. They were excited to see new faces in different uniforms and eager to know how the war was going- as if we were battle-hardened veterans needing their special form of TLC. A no-brainer for marines. We accepted the role.

Some of the doctor types were wary of our motives, yet most were making every effort to welcome us. I asked if any were from Arkansas. No luck. Plenty to drink with no bar tab, entertaining company, complimentary meals, and upgrade to hospital ward beds was our reward for just gracing the ranch with our presence. We were in hog heaven.

We were told the Commanding Colonel; a heavy-set middle-aged doctor lived in the only house on site, had a disturbing habit. He possessed a bass drum that, after getting a snoot-full each evening, he proceeded to beat into the wee hours. Outranking everyone in sight, he could damn well do what he pleased. It was there I first heard *"The natives are restless tonight."*

He invited the three of us to accompany him on a wild bear hunt the next morning. George and I declined but Jim accepted and met the colonel at the proper time. They hunted in jeeps-very non-regulation- and fired at some between libations, but returned empty handed. By then George and I were happily living our new roles in the camaraderie of the O-Club. As our listeners appeared to find our most routine duty activities interesting, we didn't have to be too inventive.

That evening we took three of the more adventuresome nurses to dinner at the Kona Club on the western shore. A drive down to the forested lowlands, three to the seat in a 1940 Ford was an interesting experience after six months on Johnston Island. Good ole boy me had never heard of Kona coffee and asked for iced tea. They found some. The drum beat had started by time we returned to base.

Next morning we knew we couldn't complete our planned trip around the island, and departed for

Hilo and the flight back to Oahu. The trip was a blur to me. I think Jim and I slept all the way.

Two weeks later we were aboard the USS Tangier, upon which we became *Trusty Shellbacks* crossing the equator and *Order of the Purple Dragon* crossing the International Date Line, en route to the Solomon Islands to finally start earning our keep.

George retired a fill colonel and Jim a Lt. Colonel, as did I. They are both deceased, but every time we were together later the conversation always got around to *The Ranch*- providing our wives were not present.

Oh, the cattle ranch? I don't recall seeing a single steer, or even thinking of one.

Semper Fi!

July 2006

Marvin Stokes

—Courtesy of Henry Stokes

CHAPTER XXII
THE MYSTERIOUS DISAPPEARANCE OF SERGEANT MARVIN STOKES, USA ARMY AIR FORCE; 1944

Plus "My Thoughts"

JUNE 19, 1944 AT 11:20 A.M. WAS THE DATE AND TIME THAT Marvin Stokes vanished. His bomber was shot down over the Channel Islands (Guernsey, Jersey, and Alderney). Alderney Island is where he landed. Five or seven parachutes left the plane according to a report from fellow American bombers. The Channel Islands were held by the Germans for most of WWII. They are between England and France.

A radio picture from the Nazi Propaganda office in Lisbon, Portugal shows the (10) flyers at Alderney with their hands in the air. It appeared on July 11, 1944 in the New York Daily News. By being captured and under guard the Red Cross should have been notified; however, the Red Cross was not on the island of Alderney. The Red Cross was the only way to find out about identified, unidentified, captured POWs, or missing in action (MIA). In many cases, partisans shot down hid flyers from the Germans. At this time the island was being blockaded by the British fleet. No food or supplies were allowed in until December 27, 1944.

What happened to Marvin Stokes and his fellow airmen? Thanks to my friend Henry Stokes, Marvin's nephew, he allowed me to view Stokes family letters about Marvin's disappearance. I viewed one letter from Marvin and one letter from Marvin's fellow airman's distraught father. The mystery touched my feelings and my heart.

"My Thoughts"

On Veterans handling of closure and their Families Memories

During WWII closure was very important. Not knowing what happened to your loved one- created stress and anxiety. The Marvin Stokes story is a mystery rolled up in a riddle.

Many WWII veterans will talk to me about what happened. Some, like the late combat Marine, Tony Muscarella, told me everything that happened. Others will tell me about some things that happened, but not the most painful. Tears for their fallen friends will appear occasionally in their eyes. This happens usually when they recall the bloody combat action. Other WWII combat veterans and some American POWs, will not talk about any of the battle actions. It is too painful and we should always respect their personal decisions of what and what not to remember and talk about.

Many have some depression when thinking about their lost combat brothers. Some slept in foxholes together to keep from freezing during the "Battle of the Bulge", which lasted forty days and forty nights starting on December 15, 1944. Some had memories of survival by taking the ammunition, weapons, clothes, and food off their dead comrades. "Night Hunting" by starving 3rd Army combat troops, who killed and stripped Germans, was prevalent. It frightened the Germans when they found eight or ten naked comrades in the snow at breakfast during the "Battle of the Bulge." Many 3rd Army veterans will not ever forget the winter of 1944&1945. It is still hard for some combat vets to make a male friend because so many of their close male friends were killed in combat during WWII.

Nazi Propaganda picture of Marvin Stokes. The captured American Airmen on Alderney Island.

—Courtesy of Henry Stokes

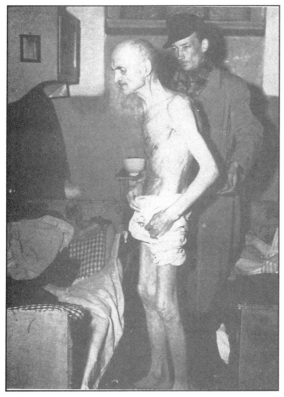

A prisoner of the Nazi for eight long years.
—Courtesy of The Lightning: The History of the 78th Infantry Division

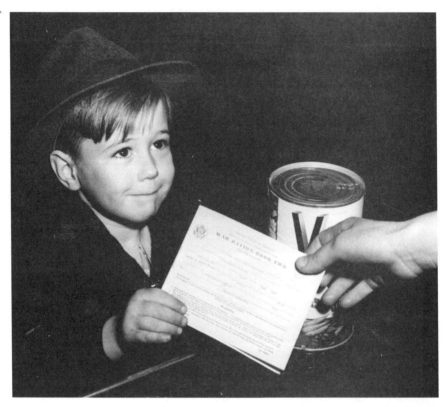

"An eager school boy gets his first experience in using war Ration Book Two."
—*Courtesy of National Archives*

CHAPTER XXIII
THE B24 "BLACK SPY PLANE"

Story of Gene Johnson

AMERICAN AIR FORCE RETIRED LIEUTENANT COLONEL Gene Johnson flew 35 combat missions during World War II. His 8th Air Force squadron flew B24's that were painted jet black, and had no nose machine gun or ball turret machine gun under the plane. The bombardier stayed in the nose of the plane behind plexi glass. He and the navigator used detailed maps to make night SPY drops. A big hole where the ball turret was supposed to be was called the "Joe Hole." American OSS spies who were to coordinate the French Resistance were pushed out of the "Joe Hole" on D Day. The "Cross of Loraine" arm bands with the French tri color (red, white, and blue) were also dropped to the Resistance Fighters. Allied troops could easily recognize the Resistance Fighters by the French arm bands.

Gene was an engineer and top turret gunner for his black B24. Only ultra violet lights and ultra violet watches were used on the black spy plane. One night, a German two engine night fighter flew a while beside Gene's right wing. The German pilot never saw his black B24. Gene asked his pilot for permission to shoot it down. The pilot said that unless you are fired on, do not shoot at the German plane.

Gene's B24 did have landing lights for use in returning to England. Supplies, ammo, and plastic explosives were also dropped to the Dutch, Belgium, and French underground. Flash lights (blinking the Morse code), white lanterns (for dropping in detailed zones), and dead reckoning were used to night drop. Uninhabited areas, wooded, with large open pastures were the best night drop areas.

One night the bombardier and pilot argued with the navigator after a night drop near Lyon. Flying time wise, they were looking too early for a lake but picked the wrong one the navigator said correctly. On the way back to England, they saw a big city and then they flew mistakenly 200 feet over Paris right by the Eiffel Tower. The German's lit up the sky with tracer bullets and 88 cannons after Gene's plane passed. It looked like fireworks. The German Anti Aircraft gun crews thought that Gene's plane was a British pathfinder leading a squadron.

A canister the size of a "small hot water tank" was crammed full with whatever the Resistance needed. It was then dropped. Some of Gene's squadron, who were flying low, hit the mountains mistakenly. This happened in the southeast section of France. Some survived and some unfortunately died.

In 1993 Gene visited with the WWII French Resistance fighters. They had their reunion in Lyon, France. One French female partisan member visited with an American flyer that had been badly burned. She had pulled him out of his Black B24 that had mistakenly hit a mountain. He was the only survivor of that eight man crew. Tears and emotions filled the room when she met him for the first time since WWII!

Air Force General, Jimmy Doolittle, cleared the sky of most German fighters in 1944. He wanted them destroyed in the air and on their bases.

Gene's squadron members were called "Carpet Baggers." One night they were supposed to make a drop to the French underground at Lyon train depot. The brazen French underground even got the Depot lights turned on. Unfortunately, an informer tipped the Germans off. Gene said that the Germans put many machine gun holes in his plane over Lyon. It was a night with tracers and fireworks. He also said it was very scary. He was actually over the bomb bay doors, with no parachute on his body. Gene was trying to push a canister of supplies out the bomb bay doors during the fireworks.

In 1972 Gene retired and later flew Falcons for Federal Express. I interviewed him in the early 1990s. His WWII oral history is fascinating.

Military Police

—Courtesy of National Archives

Danny Kaye, well known stage and screen star, entertains 4,000 5th Marine Division occupation troops at Sasebo, Japan. The crusade sign across the front of the stage says: officer's keep out! Enlisted men's country.

—*Courtesy of National Archives*

CHAPTER XXIV
THE DOUGLAS DAUNTLESS (THE NAVY CALLED IT S.B.D.- SCOUT BOMBER DOUGLAS)

Story of Simon "Spider" Webb

"SPIDER" WAS HIS COMBAT SQUADRON CALL SIGN. IT stuck for a lifetime. "Spider" Webb was from Helena, Arkansas. He graduated from high school in 1936 and attended Notre Dame two years. Then, he transferred to Ole Miss in 1939 after laying out a year, where he met his future wife, Dorothy Ann. She was from Laurel, MS.

In July of 1941, Spider enlisted in a naval flight school. He made some choices and ended up in Marine Corp Aviation. He was assigned to the first Marine Air Wing and eventually became a captain. The Air Group was formed at Goleta, CA, in June 1942, it departed San Diego by ship in January 1943 for Oahu. The air group then departed Oahu by ship for Efate, New Hebrides in September 1943. Efate was a rear base for Marine Corps dive bomber squadrons operating in the Solomons. Spider's first Marine Air Wing supported the 3rd Marine Division's activities in the Solomon Islands.

Spider was a member of the VMSB (Marine Scout Bomber Squadron) 243. The Squadron was in combat from November of 1943 through October of 1944. It covered an area roughly in the Northwest Solomons from Rabaul, to Guadalcanal in the Southeast Solomons.

Spider did three tours of duty. He took his R&R in Sydney, Australia. Chapter XX is a short story that Spider wrote himself. It is about the famous Australian Eighth Brigade's welcoming home parade, Spider was there. It touched my heart when I read about what actually happened to the Eighth Brigade on its long and tenuous travels. Spider's article is very heart warming about the Eighth Brigade's courage. He also let me include chapter XXI, The Ranch, a short story that he wrote about Hawaii

American service men took Atabrine to ward off Malaria. The British ingested Quinine to keep Malaria at bay. The Australians said they simply drank more beer as a preventative for Malaria. Atabrine would color the Americans skin with a yellow tan.

Coast watchers or air patrols were the best way to keep up with the Japanese troop and ship movements. Maps of the Solomons were not correct on many occasions. Prior to WWII National Geographic had not visited many of the remote Solomon islands. The movies *South Pacific* (planter from near Bougainville) and *Mother Goose* (spy Cary Grant) explain the importance of coast watchers in the Solomon Islands. Island planters and natives would relay ship movements by radio to the American, British, or Australian naval intelligence. This information targeted Japanese ships, troops, and air movements near their plantations or nearby islands. Spiders Air Wing would get the information and detach squadrons to attack the Japanese ships. A surprise attack was the key to defeating the Japanese.

Spider flew combat missions against the Japanese from Henderson Field, on Guadalcanal; Munda Point on New Georgia; Piva Yoke on Bougainville; and Green Island. Bougainville was not safe because of the Japanese army using artillery hidden in the mountains and shelling Piva Yoke Airfield. Spider's squadron moved on to Green Island away from the fireworks.

Rabaul was a huge Japanese supply base; it had a deep sea harbor and fortress garrison of 80,000 Japanese. McArthur simply leap frogged over it and cut it off by sea blockade. Then the Allies just bombed the hell out of it. Spider's Squadron 243 dove from the North side over some hills. He pulled out into the harbor and weaved through tracers, zigzagging through into the main channel. The Squadron lost two planes but successfully hit their target. Sylvester "Sal" Garalski from Detroit was Spider's gunner and radio operator. He and Spider bonded well and flew together for two years.

Spider recalled to me that dive bombing was tricky! You dive from approximately 12,000 feet at a 70 degree angle, canopy open, goggles on, 50 caliber machine guns blazing and watch the altimer (altitude gage): start yelling, drop the 500 pound bomb at 1500 feet, pull out at 500 feet, and get the hell out of there. The yelling keeps your ears from plugging and from blacking out. Spider was an expert and I did not write down all the other things he said you had to do, so dive bombing was very challenging.

Spider was promoted to Marine Lieutenant Colonel in 1953. He transferred to the Army Reserve in 1956 to acquire retirement points. Spider worked for U.S. Plywood from '65-'83. This was a division of Champion International Corp, later purchased by International Paper. They had a plant located near Oxford, MS. I met Spider at St.Peter's Episcopal Church in Oxford, MS. He is an active member of the church. He has two children Tom and Sally.

"Spider's" Marine combat missions helped end the war with Japan in the South Pacific. He has a keen sense of humor. Spider is a very brave American. We should all try to emulate him.

Hank Brukardt

CHAPTER XXV
THE TRANSPORT NAVIGATOR

Journal by Hank Brukardt

Tour of Duty—Casablanca, Italy, France, and England:

We flew along with many other C-87's and their crews on flights to Africa. We most often did not know our cargo. We flew by celestial over the Atlantic to Casablanca in North Africa, Italy, and France. We flew about 4 flights a month. After 6 months we moved to Metfield for flights over German occupied Norway. We had an entirely new crew there. But before we left St.Mawgan, we had to go to London to get civilian clothing. For Sweden was supposedly neutral, and we had to change into civilian clothes before leaving our planes upon landing in Stockholm. Our crew went to London, and we were billeted in a hotel, each with their room. That night, about 2 A.M., suddenly the building shook, the windows rattled, the blinds rolled up, the noise of bombs bursting, the sky was full of searchlight, the ack-ack was booming—I woke from a sound sleep and found myself on my knees on the floor before God. It was a terrifying experience.

After moving to Metfield, my other crew was never seen by me again.

Tour of Duty- England to Stockholm, Sweden:

On this new assignment we made flights over Norway to Sweden always at night. These 10 missions over enemy territory accounted for Air Medals and Oak Leaf clusters. On one flight returning to England, we were nearly over the coast when the plane shuddered noticeably. German anti-aircraft bombs were exploding all around us. Our pilot made evasive action in every direction and altitude, at which the instruments were turning and navigation was impossible until things turned to normal. Only the crew chief could look out the rear for he had no need for light. We had to keep the nose curtained from view. That is an eerie feeling, we escaped unscathed. Aside from this our worst enemy was the weather. We had perfect, nearly, navigation with British Loran, but it was good only to the Norwegian coast. From there on our navigation was D.R., dead reckoning, instruments, and predicted winds from meteorology. On one such flight we were going east over Norway. From there, you turned due south by instrument. For a certain length of time you would keep this heading by D.R., estimate your turn again to due east to Stockholm. As we were flying East we ran into a blizzard. We wondered how we would ever find Stockholm. To miss Stockholm was to immediately be over the cold, frozen Baltic Sea. As our ETA for Stockholm drew near, the clouds of the storm brightened greatly, so we had to consider these were the lights of the city. Our pilot did an instrument let-down, circling the lighted clouds. When we were about 100 feet or so, we spied a hole in the clouds and saw the airport beneath us. Suddenly the left wing just barely missed the radio tower, but we made it; anxiety.

Tour of Duty- Luleo, Sweden:

Just as suddenly, we got orders to go to Scotland. Ten crews were assigned to 10 C-47's, Gooney Birds. With brand new crews, we left Scotland and flew to Luleo, Sweden. We were stationed there until the war was nearly over. Our C.O. was Col. Bernt Balchen. We didn't know until later, and he didn't tell us, that he was Admiral Byrd's co-pilot to the South Pole, and also flew many other missions with him. We carried cargo and Norwegian troops to the Arctic Circle. On one flight, we just happened to be the only crew of the ten that found our destination, due to inclement weather. The Russians and Norwegians controlled the area. We just happened to see a hole in the clouds, and the airport was below us. We landed and unloaded our cargo. We couldn't understand the Russians nor could they understand us. When we were to take off, the Russians just kept standing in the runway. We were parked in a parking-taxi area, a small area. Our pilot, Lt. Wahrmund, braked the plane, revved the engines and we took off from the parking strip. It was the fastest near vertical takeoff I've seen.

On the way back to Luleo, we spotted a German fighter bomber, a JU'88. We were not comfortable with him in the area, but the guns on the JU-88 were elevated slightly, so that the plane had to get below you to fire at you. So we took the plane down to tree top as close as possible. Sometimes Lt. Wahrmund would have to raise a wing above an exceptionally tall tree. We radioed back to the base our situation. The JU-88 finally left the vicinity. After we landed, we were informed that the Finns had JU-88's with similar markings to the Germans.

Col. Balchen would take us on cross-country skiing. Skis became our standard baggage. The Swedes could seemingly ski faster on the flat than we could down hill. This exercise was part of our training in case we were forced down. One sentence in Swedish that we had to learn was – Vil ni visa vegen til Luleo. It may not be spelled right but it meant—will you show me the way to Luleo?

Upon leaving Sweden, I was sent to navigate another crew and plane back to the States. We left England in a C-54, I believe. We flew to Dakar, Africa and from this point on the west coast of Africa we were destined for Bermuda. It was a daylight flight, relying on sunline navigation, metro winds, drift reading of the ocean waves. Reading a driftmeter over water is conflicting, sometimes you seem to get opposite readings. And so we trusted the forecast winds, read our compasses and instruments with shots of the sun. To get an accurate fix you need three azimuths, the sunlines give only one. When our ETA for Bermuda was due, Bermuda was not yet in sight. I started to chart a square search pattern, but suddenly we saw Bermuda about 30 miles off to our right. That was a great relief.

While in flight to Bermuda, we heard the news on the radio—V.E. DAY! We arrived in Florida finally, and were given a short leave. My new wife met me in Milwaukee and we spent a few days there with relatives. We then went to Memphis onto our new assignment at Nashville. We had a belated honeymoon in Nashville. After about a week I was due to go overseas again. So Dot went back to Memphis, and I took off on a flight that day. Right after take-off, our No. 3 engine was on fire. There were many on board, and all faces were etched with fear, an ashen look. What seemed like hours, we turned back to make an emergence landing, fire trucks and ambulances lined the runway. We landed somehow without incident. Our departure delayed, Dot returned to Nashville. We had a few more hours together. As per usual, fliers had to have periodical physical exams. Mine was due, and the physician could possibly sense war weariness, and suggested he could operate on my nose and straighten it to improve my breathing. This was very tempting, for the war could be over for me. But I could not do that.

So once again we departed for Europe. Upon arrival I was assigned to navigate a B-17 with returning fliers from the tour of duties in bomb groups. Here is where we meet that pilot from the past who reminds you of Barney Fife. He was a likable fellow, but it was an exercise in fearful chance every time he flew a plane. He nearly crashed us two or three times. Once when we arrived from Stockholm, we were directly over our home base in Metfield, but we were in overcast down to 300 feet visibility. Instead of making a procedural let down he kept looking for openings in the weather. He unconsciously pulled the stick back and stalled out our C-87. The only thing left to do was to push the nose down to gain speed. We came out below the 300 ft. ceiling. The radio operator and I were lifted out of our seats. He had the look of death on his face, and he told me that I did also. He was reported to the C.O. The other crew members stated no confidence in him. He pleaded with me to not go along with their report. I went along with his request, and now I have this pilot to fly back to the states with. We took off with capacity loading of everything, including fuel. With this overload, we took off and had to make a quick stop at Wales. This pilot nearly put the left wing on the ground on his final turn. I didn't sleep for the next two days. We left Wales and landed: Reyjavik, Iceland. There we had to wait for the weather and night flight for celestial navigation. Upon leaving there we flew all night, landing at Bangor, Me. I was exhausted. We got out of the plane, put all our gear on the ground. I don't remember if I kissed the ground or did so in my mind. I sat against the gear and fell asleep. We were awakened and taken to a hotel in town. We all phoned home, but I don't believe any of us heard the phones ring. Again we were awakened and had to report to the train station bound for Chicago. This would be great. We would get a ringside seat and see New England, New York, Pennsylvania, Ohio, and Indiana. After ten minutes on the train, the conductor woke us in Chicago. We changed trains for Milwaukee. The conductor woke us up in the depot in Milwaukee. There was a hotel next to the depot. We billeted there, gathered all our gear and called home again. We woke up the next afternoon.

Our orders read to report to Hamilton Field, San Francisco, Cal., with a 30 day delay enroute. Dot and I spent a few days in Wisconsin, went to Memphis, and found a '39 Chevy for $900. We took off in September to California. It was very warm in Memphis, but in Colorado, Rabbit Ears Pass was closed. It was snowing high in the Colorado Rockies, a picture book phantasy at 2 A.M. It was picture post card beautiful.

Upon arrival in California, after reporting in, we found a place to stay in San Rafael. I was ordered to take a flight and navigate to Hickam Field, Hawaii. On this flight, I had about all a person could take, by this time. Without others knowing it, I bawled like a baby. My nerves were shot. It so happened we were sent back to California. Upon arrival we were proud to see orders to go to Sacramento for separation. The war for us was over.

Chapter 2 Where From Here

We went to Milwaukee where we tried to get a little grocery store, but that did not come to pass. With advice from Uncle George we bought a small house on 53rd Street. I worked for a construction millwork company, on the G.I. bill. But after 6 months of hard winter we went to Memphis. I worked in three companies as a draftsman and designer for a fabricating company. These first three companies I worked for were found defrauding the government on the G.I. bill.

Things were not going well and I had a bad case of war nerves. Nothing seemed to go right, and I became very depressed. In fact, I went to the V.A. hospital in Memphis and asked the psychiatrist to put me in the hospital ward. I feared for my sanity, and felt that life was done. It was the darkest days of my life. I told Dot I was going to Milwaukee. I took a Greyhound bus and had a 3 hour layover in Chicago. I thought any minute I would explode. Upon arrival in Milwaukee and getting with my brother and a friend, that helped the strain. Red was getting married and so they were moving out of the apartment. I helped them move and as I was upstairs alone, it seemed that the devil whispered loudly, why don't you just take those ties and hang yourself. I immediately left, got on a bus back to Memphis , and had to lay over again in Chicago. I was very glad to get back to Memphis. One evening at an evening service at First Baptist Church, Dot went forward at the invitation of the pastor, to receive Christ. A few months later at the same church, at the invitation of the pastor, Dr. Caudill, I too gave my heart to the Lord. The healing had begun!

Hank and Dorothy Brukardt

—*Courtesy of Hank Brukardt*

Private Roy Humphrey is being given blood plasma by Pfc. Harvey White, after he was wounded by shrapnel, on August 9, 1943 in Sicily.

—Courtesy of National Archives

—Courtesy of The Lightning: The History of the 78th Infantry Division

Spotted by the enemy, these infantrymen were forced to hit the ground for protection from flying shell fragments.

—*Courtesy of The Lightning: The History of the 78th Infantry Division*

Inspecting German 88 Damage of anti-aircraft to a B17.
Lew Lyle (on right)

—Courtesy of Mrs. Lew Lyle

CHAPTER XXVI
THE MIGHTY EIGHTH AIR FORCE

Story of Major General Lewis E. Lyle

THE USA WAS NOT MILITARILY READY FOR WORLD WAR II. Roosevelt and Churchill decided to "quick fix" a bad situation on the evening of December 7, 1941. They formed the American 8th Bomber Command. It could attack Germany and relieve pressure on England quickly. On January 28, 1942, the United States Army created the Eighth Air Force. The 303rd Wing was not ready because of logistical and personnel problems. The Wing's personnel, supplies, and planes were ferried over to England in early 1942. B17's and short range escort fighters called P 38s and P 47s were the first to arrive in England.

In March of 1942 the British began building concrete runways for the 8th Air Force. Everything the British did was unionized, done by hand, and very slow. The 8th Air Force brought over, from the USA, automated equipment, drivers, and engineers. Lew Lyle said, "The British resisted our automation at first, but we won out in the end. The 8th's first bomb raid was August 17, 1942. Six B17's hit some French railroad marshalling yards along the coast. It took time to build the 8th to a large strike force. Lew Lyle flew on the third mission of the 8th during October of 1942. Lew flew nine more combat missions before he flew a classified night mission to Casa Blanca in December 1942. He flew the 8th Air Force's Commander General Acker and his staff to Casa Blanca by way of Gibraltar.

"Churchill and Roosevelt came early to the Casa Blanca Conference to discuss Precision Daylight Bombing." Lew said: General Acker made the pitch to Roosevelt and Churchill. Churchill agreed to the idea of total twenty four hour air war. Churchill said total war is the British bombing at night and the Americans precision bombing during the day.

On August 17, 1943, the German key ballbearing factory located at Schweinfurt, Germany was heavily bombed by the 8th Air Force. The 8th also bombed the German submarine pens at Bordeaux, France. They were targeted with concrete piercing bombs. My French wine (negotiate) friend, Mr. Nathaniel Johnston, told me a German U Boat is still sealed up in its watery river grave at Bordeaux. His office is on the Quay (river bank) in Bordeaux. He also told me that the French Resistance would kill German River Guards and concrete them completely in new bridges. This helped shot down Aviators escape by water easier.

Lewis said, " we were losing until General Jimmy Doolittle took over as commander of the 8th in February of 1944."

Doolittle asked the 8th Air Force members to give him a "Total Effort" to destroy the German Luftwaffe. The goal was to destroy airplane producing factories, basic war, and material factories. It worked and did cripple the German Army's war material supplies and air support for the rest of the war.

Lewis said," The Eighth had a total of 350,000 stationed in England and the USA during WWII." The Eighth Aviators had 50,000 shotdown, 28,000 became POWs, and 2,500 were smuggled out by The Resistance located in Italy, France, Belgium, Holland, and Yugoslavia. Many French men and women were killed or permanently scarred by the Gestapo for helping the Eighth. Priests, farmers, and everyday working class citizens saved our young Eighth Air Force aviators from death or capture.

When an Eighth plane was shot down: Information about it's demise would be reported to a debriefer at the plane's base. Their fellow 303rd Wing crews may give different accounts of what they witnessed. The Red Cross would also get useful information from "German Reports." The reports were slow in coming to American families. When the Germans found the shot down plane, the report would read Dead-Identified, Dead-Unidentified, Captured POWs, or Missing in Action (MIA).

Their daily fly overs and "daylight precision bombing" crippled the Luftwaffe, German factories, train yards, and vital oil refineries were decimated. So many targets were destroyed, the German army ran our of gas and oil products for their tanks during the "Battle of the Bulge" (December 13, 1944). The 8th Air Force was in many ways responsible for most German shortages.

One day, in 1944, the Eighth Air Force flew into the sky 2,000 bombers and 4,000 fighters. It was a beautiful, blue sky and clear morning. Their "contrails" from the 6,000 planes soon clouded up the sky over "merry old England."

The Eighth has a fantastic WWII air museum that is located near Savannah, Georgia. I spent a full day researching there last summer. It is located just ten miles from Savannah at Puller, Georgia in Chatham County. The two United State's interstates, 80 and 90 west, take you to it. The only way to truly realize the bravery and courage of the young aviators in the Eighth is to visit the Savannah museum.

General Lewis E Lyle did over seventy missions in WWII. I consider him a B 17 Ace. He did three tours of duty.

Lew Lyle in 2000 at the Mighty 8th AirForce Museum in Savannah, Georgia.
                                              —*Courtesy of Mrs. Lew Lyle*

—Courtesy of The Lightning: The History of the 78th Infantry Division

The Assault on Schwammenauel Dam
—Courtesy of The Lightning: The History of the 78th Infantry Division

Robert Morgan and Margaret
Polk- The Memphis Belle
(B 17), 1943
—Courtesy of Edwin Frank

Lamar Wallis

—*Courtesy of Lamar Wallis*

CHAPTER XXVII
THE 69TH DIVISION'S DRIVE ACROSS GERMANY TO THE ELBE RIVER

Story of C. Lamar Wallis

IT ALL STARTED IN CAMP SHELBY, MS. IN WORLD WAR I there was a fighting 69th Regiment. When we got into World War II, it was renamed the fighting 69th Division; both generations liked to fight and win.

C. Lamar Wallis, was a Sergeant Major in the 273rd Infantry Regiment of the 69th Division. They did their basic training at Camp Shelby, MS. He marched the 69th's New York City and New Jersey Recruits for twenty five miles one day in the summer heat and mud. Lamar told me "many fell out because they were not use to our summer heat and humidity."

Europe: In the Huertgen Forest of Germany, near the Ziegfried Line, Lamar said an American P38 strafed the 69th Division twice. Friendly fire is dangerous, especially since the Battle Lines are sometimes so close. Lamar told me that "He had to get behind a large tree twice. The P38 did successfully destroy their food and mess tent near the Ziegfried Line.

At Marmady the 69th Division viewed four GI's shot, execution style, in the forehead while in the snow. For weeks the Germans paid dearly for this atrocity.

Screaming Mimi's were sent at the 69th's Division by German Artillery. Captain Paris, of M Company, did not duck and was killed by one Lamar said. The shell makes a noise like a woman screaming and unnerves soldiers."

The 69th Division captured Aachen, Germany, where Charlemagne, the Emperor, is buried. Lamar said, "it was torn up."

Battle of Fort Erin Bronstein: An American Officer of the 69th Division got lost near there and finally stopped in to get a haircut in a German barbershop. The barber set up a dinner that evening with the local German commander. After a telephone call to Berlin, much wine and food the German commanders surrendered his 1,200 man garrison to the fighting 69th Division. Many lives were saved by this German barber's help.

Battle of Leipzig, Germany: At the City Hall the 69th Division found the Burgermeister and his wife and daughter dead of ingesting poison. Lamar said, "The University of Leipzig was in total rubble from American Artillery and air raids." Lamar found a German "Hitler glorified" book in a 2nd floor room that he occupied during the street fighting. Each German soldier received a similar propaganda book.

The German S.S. Garrison was ensconced up in an enormous monument called the Nation's Monument. It had fourteen feet thick. The S.S. had a 105 mm cannon firing from the top of the Nation's Monument. They took it up there by use of an elevator.

Seventeen of the 69th Division's GI's had been taken prisoner in the street fighting near the Monument. They were from Company F. The S.S. jailed them inside the Monument that day. A white flag of truce was called by both sides. A dinner of wine and food was served to the American and German commander inside the Monument. While dining, an American Army Harvard professor(translator and bilingual) talked the S.S. commander into surrendering. What a life saver!

Nederland: At the Stein Spa town of Nederland, Lamar's unit found a huge champagne and wine cellar under the hotel that they occupied. They needed to shave but had no running water or electricity. Lamar said: "We lathered up with shaving cream and poured champagne into sinks and it shaved us perfectly." We immediately dumped our "paper personnel records" out of its truck to make room for more champagne. The champagne helped the 69th in many ways.

Elbe River: The 69th Division and the Russians met at the Elbe River. Lieutenant Robinson of the 69th was seen greeting them in most Allied newspapers.

Lamar received the bronze star and was chief warrant officer of the 69th Division when he was discharged. He is retired and resides in Memphis, TN. Enclosed is some of the bio he recently sent me.

WALLIS, CARLTON LAMAR, librarian; b. Blue Springs, Miss., Oct. 15, 1915; s. William Ralph and Tellie (Jones) W.; m. Mary Elizabeth Cooper, Feb. 22, 1944; 1 child, Carlton Lamar. BA with spl. distinction, Miss. Coll., 1936; MA, Tulane U., 1946; B.L.S., U. Chgo., 1947; L.H.D., Rhodes Coll., Memphis, 1980. English tchr., coach Miss. Pub. Schs., 1936-41; teaching fellow Miss. Coll. and Tulane U., 1941-42; chief librarian Rosenberg Library, Galveston, Tex., 1947-55; city librarian Richmond, Va., 1955-58; dir. Memphis Pub. Library, 1958-80, ret., 1980. Author: Libraries in the Golden Triangle, 1966; contbr. articles to library jours. Trustee Belhaven Coll., 1978-82, Nat. Ornamental Metal Mus., 1989–. Served as chief warrant officer AUS, 1942-46. Decorated Bronze Star. Mem. ALA (chmn. library mgmt. sect. 1969-71), Pub. Library Assn. (dir. 1973-77), Tex. Library Assn. (pres. 1952-53), Va. Library Assn., Southwestern Library Assn. (exec. bd. 1950-55), Southeastern Library Assn. (chmn. pub. library sect. 1960-62), Tenn. Library Assn. (pres. 1969-70, Distinguished Service award 1979, Intellectual Freedom award 1998). Presbyterian (elder). Club: Egyptian (pres. 1973-74).

Lamar Wallis

—Courtesy of Lamar Wallis

Bitter, penetrating cold was a much of an enemy as the men in gray-green.

—*Courtesy of The Lightning: The History of the 78th Infantry Division*

Linden Wright

CHAPTER XXVIII
"MINE SWEEPING TO YALTA"
Story of Linden Wright

LINDEN WRIGHT, A RETIRED NAVAL COMMANDER, SPENT twenty six years in the reserve and ten years of active duty. Linden left college during WWII and joined the V7 program and attended Mid Shipman School in Chicago. He spent 90 days in the school. He served on the Wichita as his first training ship.

Linden's first assignment was to sweep Newfoundland of mines and check for U-Boat activity. His ship got into a bad North Eastern storm in the Atlantic. Linden said that water came into the bridge and pilot house of his ship near Newfoundland.

Linden was in a convoy going to England in a wooden hull mine sweeper with only a 6' draft. He said," The engine Conked Out" and it wallowed in the Atlantic waves for six to ten hours. The convoy left. Thank God no U-Boats were close by. They finally got her running and made it to merry old England.

Linden said," A U Boat sent a torpedo at his ship near Marseille, France. Fortuantely, he was in the same wooden hull mine sweeper with which only took a 6' water draft in the Mediterranean Sea. The torpedo went under the ship and totally missed it.

In Sicily Linden bought supplies of food and wine for the "wooden hull" mine sweeper. It was anchored and being loaded. He was taking in the last of a thirty-day supply when a German plane dropped a bomb on the Harbor's pier. Fortunately, the bomb missed his ship but made a mess of the pier and the wine.

He was transferred to a new steel hulled mine sweeper. This ship went through the Dardanelles, near Constantinople (Istanbul.) This was the first U.S. ship sent to enter the Black Sea to clear mines. He was also the executive officer of this ship. The Catachtin, a U.S. cruiser, was the communication ship for this conference. He also had signal corp personnel aboard this ship. It was to prepare the way for the coming Yalta Conference.

In February 1945 he went to the Yalta Conference. Yalta is a town in the Crimea. The conference was at the Czar's summer palace. Stalin, Churchill, and Roosevelt attended the Yalta Conference. Molotov of Russia, King Evonsol of Iran, and King Faroudt of Egypt also attended this conference. Linden said, " Later on Stalin reneged on his pledge of free elections for Soviet occupied territory. He also told me Poland was given to Russia. Churchill smelled a "skunk" in future dealings with Stalin, but was overruled two to one. Roosevelt was sick and died within ninety days.

He was also the executive officer of this ship.

Linden told me that he extricated, from the Russians, a sailor from his ship who was in trouble. The family of a young Russian girl said that the American sailor had taken advantage of her youth.

At Yalta Local teachers told Linden that the Germans had drowned box cars of Russians at Sebastopol. They simply rolled the box car into the water. The Catachtin, a U.S. cruiser, was the communication ship for this conference.

Linden showed me an Argonaut directory of the Dardanelles, Yalta and Sebastopol. I really still don't know what it contained or it's use.

Linden's WWII journal is safely kept at the Memphis Public Library.

Linden Wright

—*Courtesy of Janet Wright*

Yalta Conference

—*Courtesy of National Archives*

CHAPTER XXIX
GUADALCANAL
Story of Bill Fisher

I SUGGEST YOU READ *PACIFIC WAR* BY JOHN COSTELLO before you read this oral history of Bill Fisher's experiences.

Guadalcanal means "many rivers" in French. This autobiography story is from Bill Fisher (a retired Second Marine Division, Raider Battalion Major.) Bill said there are 4,700 American sailors, black and white, that died and are entombed in sunken ships near Guadalcanal. About twenty four ships each were lost by the Americans and the Japanese.

Let's tumble back in history a little bit. Bill Fisher was from Covington, TN. He was sixteen years old when he enlisted in the Marines. Bill told me that was put in the brigade in Hawaii for misbehaving. I do not know the details on this.

Bill joined the Second Marine Division Raider Battalion. They were sent to their training base, in the New Hebrides Islands, which are located near the East of Australia and South of the Solomons. Bill trained off of submarines. From there they were sent to Guadalcanal in the Solomon Islands. Incidentally, James Roosevelt, FDR's son, was a Marine raider in Bill's battalion.

Bill's raiders came up with the idea of four in a fire team instead of nine. You would have one director of fire and three shooting.

Bill carried sixty pounds of machine gun ammunition during his trek through Guadalcanal. Later on in life, Bill had to have both knee caps replaced at the Veterans Hospital in Memphis, TN because of this heavy load of ammunition. The new knee caps were made by Smith and Nephew.

At 6:06 am, August 7, 1942, a Japanese radio observation station sent a message to Rabual. The message read "Unidentified naval task force observed off Guadalcanal." At 6:07 a.m. the U.S. Cruiser Quincy began the American Naval barrage that destroyed their Japanese radio observation station. The Southern part of Guadalcanal is all mountains. The Northern part of the island is a plain where the Battle took place.

The Allied surprise attack and the use of logistics eventually won the battle. Bill Fisher said to me, "Once you are in combat and you realize that you are the person he is trying to kill, that becomes the most important battle."

On August 21, 1942 at the Battle of Alligator Creek the Japanese were stopped. The Ichiki detachment, including Ichiki himself tried to overrun U.S. Lines. Over 277 bodies, including Ichiki , were found on the morning of August 21, 1942. They were found sprawled in a death sleep on the sandpit of Alligator Creek. Ichiki apparently had committed suicide after his attacks failed.

The Battle of Bloody Ridge took place September 12,13, and 14, 1942. The Allies killed 800 Japanese at Bloody Ridge. It was a great show of U.S. firepower. Bloody Ridge at Henderson Field(called the cow pasture) saved the day for the Americans. 21,000 Japanese troops were killed in the battle for Guadalcanal. Twenty six Japanese war ships rest in the deep waters off Guadalcanal, with uncounted crew members entombed. Six hundred and eighty Japanese Aircraft, with 1,800 crew members, were scattered over the Guadalcanal area of battle.

The American losses were staggering. The U.S. Navy had over 5,000 men killed, two aircraft carriers sunk, and twenty two warships. The Army, Navy and Marine Aircraft, lost by the Americans were 615. There were 420 American Airmen killed in action. Over 1,592 American Marine and Army troops were killed. The Second Marine Division lost 774 dead of that total.

Bill Fisher told me that Guadalcanal was a logistics nightmare; this was for both the Japanese and the Allies. He saw cereal boxes of Kellogg's corn flakes floating in the bay nearby.

In 1994 Bill went back to visit the Bloody Ridge. He remembered capturing one Japanese off of a small patrol boat. There were, according to Bill, 15,000 cases of severe malaria in and around Guadalcanal. He recovered from it himself. From the interview with Bill he mentioned a lieutenant Clifton Cates (later Commander of the Corps) and a Battalion Commander named Colonel Hannigan. He also said the Japanese were very rigid and many starved to death.

On his 1994 visit to Guadalcanal the natives reported that dead bodies wash up after storms from their tombs on the sunken ships occasionally.

Bill visited Guadalcanal five times during his life after World War II. Some of his ashes are scattered over Guadalcanal.

Jim McWillie

—*Courtesy of Jim McWillie*

CHAPTER XXX
THE POWERFUL B26 MARTIN
MARAUDER- MEDIUM BOMBER

Story of Jim McWillie

JIM WAS MARRIED AT ST. ANN'S CATHOLIC CHURCH ON February 12, 1942 in his hometown, Memphis, TN. He volunteered for the Army Air Corp in May of 1942 at the age of 27.

Jim completed his basic training for Glider Pilot. Gliders were temporarily pulled from combat in 1943. He was reclassified at Keesler Air Field and sent to Scott Field for training as a Radio Operator and to Ft. Meyer's, Florida for Aerial Gunnery training.

Jim served aboard the Martin B26 Marauder and The Douglas A26 during his WWII tours of duty.

The B26 was built in Baltimore, Maryland by the Martin Aircraft Factory. It was grounded by congress and Harry Truman because of electrical, low voltage, propeller and engineering problems. They called the plane the "Widow Maker" and "One a Day in Tampa Bay." One plane a day was crashing into Tampa Bay. Tad Hankey, a Senior Pilot and Group Operations Officer at McDill Field in Tampa, Florida, determined to prove the plane air worthy. He took a plane up to 7,000 feet altitude, lowered the Landing Gear, revved the engines and put the plane in "take-off" procedure. The plane flipped over and went into a "flat" spin. He came out of the spin and returned to normal flight, knowing what caused the failures on "take-off." Tad had solved the problems and he and Martin corrected the defects. By the end of the War, the B-26 had proved to be the most outstanding Medium Bomber in the entire European Theatre of Operations.

The B26 had a crew of six. It was equipped with twelve, 50 caliber machine guns. The A26 had eighteen 50 caliber machine guns. Both used Norton bomb sights. Jim said normally they bombed at 12,000 feet. A pathfinder led the way at times and you "copied his run."

Jim left the USA on the Queen Elizabeth I from New York City. 20,000 Soldiers were aboard the Queen Elizabeth I, heading for Scotland. The ship zigzagged all the way. U Boats were to slow to catch her. Jim said it only took five days to make the crossing.

He was assigned to the 386th Bomb Group in November 1944. Their base was at Beaumont Sur Oise, France on the outskirts of Paris. The cold winter of 1944 and 1945 hampered air support. In March the Group moved to St. Trond Belgium to be closer to their German targets. The Group remained at St. Trond Air Base after V-E Day until late July of 1945 training for the Pacific Theatre of Operations.

The 386th participated in the Mediterranean, Ardennes Battle of the Bulge, Rhineland and the Battle of Berlin campaigns. He participated in the bombing of Weisbaden, the German Western Headquarters. On that mission, his plane lost an engine and received 88 holes from anti-aircraft fire and from German Me 109's and FW 190 Fighter Planes.

Jim said our P47 Thunderbolt's (P47's) were Tank killers and the German's feared it. His group liked them because they not only provided good Fighter cover but would go down on the "deck" and take out the German's 88 Flak Guns.

On March 20, 1945, one of his most dangerous missions was an attack on the Redoubt area South West of Berlin just outside of Wittenberg. The mission was to take out a vast number of German hold-outs who refused to surrender and were committed to fight to the bitter end. Jim's pilot volunteered Jim and himself with two other crews to go ahead of the main mission at 200 feet to take out the German 88's located in three separate grove of trees. The three A-26's were armed with Anti-Personnel bombs for the action. On the bomb-run, they were so close they could see the Swastika Signs on the German helmets. On the approach as the bombs were released, ground fire took out their left engine along with bullet holes from German small arms fire.

Jim's plane flew out of the area but could not gain altitude to catch up with the Plane flying overhead to take them back to their base. They had no navigator and after a long period of time were concerned about low fuel and only one Parachute. Jim climbed through the Bomb Bay to get to the Pilot's compartment and the Radio Compass to try to get a bearing to take them home, in doing so his parachute ring caught on a Bomb shackle and blossomed his chute. When he reached the cockpit, he turned on the radio compass and located the Rheims radio call sign J88. They knew their way to the Base from Rheims and headed that way. On reaching Rheims, the compass needle did a 180 degree turn and they headed for home.

Jim McWillie
—Courtesy of Jim McWillie

On reaching St. Trond, overdue and almost out of fuel and on one engine, they landed and to their amazement, almost all of Jim's squadron were on the runway welcoming them home. Jim and his Pilot's name had already been marked on the Mission Roster as "MIA." Jim said thanks to his good Pilot, his Radio training and the Grace of God they made it back, saved their Airplane and maybe themselves.

On the day Jim arrived at Ft. McPhearson, Georgia for a thirty day leave before going to the Pacific, that very day the Atom Bomb was dropped on Japan. Jim had his furlough and on returning to Ft. McPhearson received his discharge, his War was over!

Columns of captured Wehrmacht soldiers grew longer
—*Courtesy of The Lightning: The History of the 78th Infantry Division*

Infantrymen use German trenches during a brief halt while awaiting orders to move out.

—*Courtesy of* The Lightning: The History of the 78th Lightning Division

Crawford McDonald (top row, far left)

—*Courtesy of Crawford McDonald*

CHAPTER XXXI
THE B24 PILOT AND THE END OF THE JAPANESE EMPIRE

Journal by Crawford McDonald

IN LATE 1944, CRAWFORD MCDONALD AND HIS crew trained at Muroc, California Air Base, flew a B-24 to Guam and from there were ferried to the island of Angaur, in Pelilou Islands, some dozen miles south of Babelthorpe. Angaur is also six miles south of the next southern most island of the group which is Pelilou, which the U.S. Marines had taken in a very bloody battle (Frank Glankler, Jr. and Ottos Melsa of Memphis were both in that Marine engagement). There were, at the time, some 70,000 or 80,000 Japanese on Babelthorpe, 80 miles long, the northern most island of that group. The Japanese remained bypassed for the rest of the War; however, they continually tried to build rafts and float down to attack the Americans, and our Bomb Group was charged with not only bombing the Philippines to the west, but also discouraging the Japanese to the north of us. This was the 494th Heavy Bomb Group of the Seventh Air Force.

In April of 1945, the Bomb Group started to move and by the middle of June of 1945 were ready to fly off Yontan field on Okinawa. Though, presumably the island had been secured from the Japanese defenders by that time, on several occasions Japanese who had hidden in the burial caves on the island, crept out and one time entered our bomb group living area and shot up one of our crews.

On Okinawa, the Marines had an anti-aircraft battery near Yontan Air Base, that for over two months would fire at the Betty Bombers that would fly over at about 30,000 feet to harass and seek to bomb us. Although none ever hit our field, situated a little to the northeast of Naha, the principle city on the island, which is located approximately half-way up the island on the west coast.

We frequently tuned into Tokyo Rose by radio, and also experienced visually the experience of seeing several naval ships attacked by the Divine Wind- the Japanese Kamikaze flyers. Towards the end of the war, some of the Japanese bombers carried "Baka Bombs" which had just room enough for a pilot to glide a flying bomb into a ship or another target. I later saw quite a few of these bombs at Atsugi Airfield, where I became stationed.

Some interesting statistics, the Japanese suffered some 85,000 casualties, at Okinawa, probably their largest at any location during the war. The same was true of the Americans, who suffered some 35,000 casualties. The number compares with some 13,000 to 15,000 casualties to take Iwo Jima in many ways matching the bloody battles of Pelilou, Tarawa and Guadalcanal.

With our own Divine Wind, we flew missions off Yontan Field to Shanghai to our northwest and many missions to Kyushu, plus a few southwest to Honshu.

SOME MISSION MEMORIES:

In briefing to bomb Shanghai, we were warned to absolutely drop our bombs only on the airport, since the Japanese had placed our POWs on the perimeter of the airport and if we over or under shot, we would kill some of our own people. On several missions there were virtually no Japanese fighters, but significant anti-aircraft, and as I recall we lost one or two planes to anti-aircraft.

On July 28, 1945, we sent a mission of some 12 planes to bomb Kure Harbor on Southern Honshu; in particular, to try to sink the battleship Haruna, which was in the harbor there. Unknown to us at the time, the Japanese did not have enough fuel to operate it, and it was actually sitting "in the mud." Nevertheless, our Bomb Group, plus bombers from the Navy Carrier Ticonderoga flew over and dropped their bombs, none of which apparently damaged the battleship. Several Navy planes were shot down as well as two of our bombers. One of these bombers was commanded by Tom Cartwight, who has written a book on his experiences, titled "The Lonesome Lady." Of Cartwright's crew of nine, the tail gunner bailed our first and hid out on the ridge of the mountain north of Kure and was not captured. He ran out of food and came down into Kure late in August to find out the War was already over and he got home safely. The same was true of Cartwright, who bailed out successfully. The bombardier's chute did not open, and he was killed on impact. The other six members of the crew with Cartwright were placed in a truck upon capture and taken to a prison where they were placed in a dungeon. The next day after capture, Cartwright was placed on a train and sent to Tokyo where central interrogation for intelligence purposes was made of all pilots. He was placed in the prison ward with Pappy Boyington, a famous Marine Pilot, who had shot down some 34 or 35 Japanese fighters. Cartwright survived and now lives in Utah. The final six members of the crew were in a jail/dungeon in Hiroshima approximately 2,000 feet from ground zero on August 6, 1945. On or about the next day they were taken out; one was crucified on a bridge, and the others were stoned to death. Verification of this occurrence was made by a young Japanese boy who was 12 at the time and farily badly burned by the radiation, but who at approximately age 60, put the story together and contacted the affected American's families. He said he knew that the families of these men would like to know what happened to them. In addition to this crew there was several American Navy POWs who were in the same jail/dungeon and also suffered death. Three days after Hiroshima, a B-29 "Boch's Car" dropped a second atom bomb on Nagasaki. Two days thereafter on August 11th, the 494th flew its last mission bombing from Okinawa. The crew of Crawford McDonald, by circumstances, was the last of the eighteen planes in that formation at 13,000 feet, which was scheduled to bomb an industrial city, "probably Kurume", 50 miles down wind of Nagasaki. Even at that time the smoke from the fires of Nagasaki blowing down wind covered so much of the target that the bombs were not dropped there. Needless to say, this was certainly the longest day of the war for Crew 40B of the 866th Bomb Squadron of the 494th Bomb Group since we all knew the war ought to be over, but it wasn't. To finish the mission, the Group flew south across Kyushu, never seeing an enemy fighter and experiencing no anti-aircraft fire and dropped their bombs on what was thought at the time to be a fishing village called Kagoshima. Later it was determined to be the naval base where the Japanese armada left to invade the Philippines at the beginning of the war (poetic justice)?

Still another Divine Wind, a typhoon came across Okinawa in the middle of October of 1945 and destroyed most of the 494th Bomb Group aircraft. RESULT: Since the McDonald Crew was one of the newest crews in the group, it was sent to Japan for occupation purposes. The individual crew members became the members of the Fifth Air Force and were assigned willi nilli. Crawford McDonald was allowed to choose his base and chose Atsugi, since he "was sure" McArthur who had landed there, would have only gone into a superior base. Not so, his G2 landed him in one of the worst bases, quality wise in Japan.

Now grounded, I was put in charge of spraying DDT at various locations from Hokiddo to Fukuoka on Kyushu. A Japanese interpreter was necessary and I was assigned Mr. Konzo Ohata, who became a close enough acquaintance to be asked why he spoke such fluent English. He said, "I am a graduate of UCLA." He was the middle aged son, of what could only be described as a Samurai family. Because of the shortage of food in his area in 1945, he and I drove in a jeep to his place of birth, approximately 100 miles northwest of Tokyo. His older brother, through their primo-generator law inherited everything. Younger brothers and sisters were supposed to go out and make it on their own, but if one cannot, he/she can come home and have to be taken care of by the older brother. We stayed a night at the brother's and then at the brother-in-law's. The brother-in-law questioned me: "Lieutenant, so you know General McArthur?" of course I replied that he was some five or six military grades above me and no that I had not met him. He proceeded to say:" Last week I hunted ducks with General McArthur!!. Since I was driving in an area approximately 100 miles north of Tokyo, where I was not actually cleared to go, I was so astounded I never even asked the gentlemen his name.

MISCELLANEOUS ERRATA:

My brother Percy McDonald, was a member of the Sixth Marine Division and landed on April 1, invasion day, on Okinawa. As a member of intelligence gathering unit, he fortunately was not a front line marine and so survived, although he had the good fortune to capture a Japanese. This was a very dangerous occurrence in those days, since Japanese when captured, usually tried to carry a hand grenade under their arm pits to blow up both themselves and the capturer up. By this time, the Japanese ordinance had become so poor that it frequently did not go off. In fact, my brother spent the night in a cave near Naha and they heard a large thump during the night. When they went to the entrance of the cave the next morning, there was a 20" diameter unexploded Japanese naval shell at the entrance. Later in the day, at the rear of that cave they found all of the yen of the Japanese Bank of Naha, but since they "knew" that this currency would be valueless at the end of the war (we know now that it wasn't), they didn't take even one stack of bills.

The one souvenir of substance that I was able to ship home from Japan was a rifle. It was in a warehouse near or on Atsug base. It was part of 500 rifles sent by Hitler to Hirohito when Japan declared war on the United Sates. It was delivered, I am told, by a German submarine. It is a German Mauzer rifle, 31 caliber, and I am sure it was made in Skoda works during World War II. This Czechoslovakian arms plant, commonly thought to be the largest arms manufacturing plant in the world.

UNTOLD EVENT:

Shortly after the Armistice was signed with the Japanese about September 15, 1945, the 24th Bomb Group put seals in its planes bomb bays of our planes and we ferried POWs from Japan to the Philippines, where they were placed on ships to go home. Unfortunately, with respect to the first trip made, our briefing instructions were to fly to the China (land side) of Formosa to go down to the Philippines. Unfortunately, it was not mentioned that there are mountains on Formosa up to 13,500 feet. Because of the heavy clouds of that period of the year (remember that is typhoon time in the Pacific) one of our planes decided to short circuit the trip and that plane was not found until about 20 years later on the east side of a mountain slope on Formosa. Another plane had to ditch just off the north end of the Formosa (Taiwan today) island and fortunately everyone was picked up. Everyone else was delivered safely to the Philippines, but was a horrible result since some of those people had been prisoners of war for three and one-half years. One of the men that flew with me was from Southhampton, England and had been taken a prisoner in Singapore. He was captured in the first 60 days of the war and was shipped first to China and then to Kobe, Japan. As they were leaving Shanghai by ship, an American submarine sank the ship they were on and he was one of only some 10 prisoners of war that were picked up by a Japanese vessel and therefore survived. He said that during the last 28 days of the war, not a single ship had come into Kobe harbor, so he knew the war could not last too much longer. In fact, Japanese officer's families were beginning to get so hungry that they had the POWs steal food grain for them. Naturally, that allowed the POWs to feed themselves better than would otherwise occurred. The concept of face would have required any Japanese caught doing this to commit hari-kari.

GOING HOME:

Towards the end of January, 1946, I had enough points (70) to take a ship home, I debarked at Ft. Lewis, Washington, I caught a train to Denver to meet Frances Alford, the girl I wrote virtually everyday while over seas and we became engaged. She then put me through school, obtaining not only a B.S./M.S. and LL.B., but also three sons. What a girl, what a life!

Crawford McDonald

Two U.S. soldiers on Pelilou Island.

—*Courtesy of National Archives*

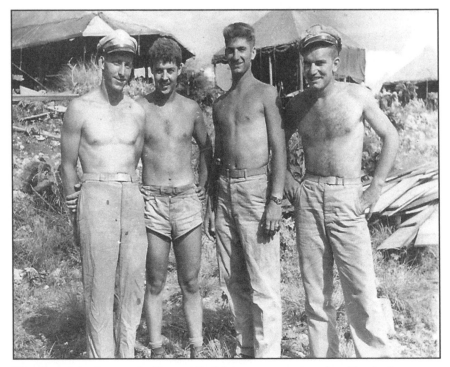

The Cartwight Crew and officers. All of these men were murdered by the Japanese except Cartwright(2nd from the left). Two of the men were stoned to death and one of the men was crucified on the bridge by Japanese civilians of Hiroshima.

—Courtesy of Crawford McDonald

Cartwright (1992)The only survivor from the crew mentioned in the above picture.
—Courtesy of Crawford McDonald

Crawford was assigned an interpreter, Mr. Konzo Ohata. He went with Mr. Ohata to his brother's house which was approximately 100 miles northwest of Tokyo.

—Courtesy of Crawford McDonald

The next home that Crawford and Mr. Ohata stayed at was that of Mr. Ohata's brother in law(which is pictured below).(Crawford is fourth from the left, with the hat on)

—Courtesy of Crawford McDonald

Okinawa (Crawford's B-24 living area)
—*Courtesy of Crawford McDonald*

Destroying small arms.-
Japan, August 30, 1945
—*Courtesy of National Archives*

Crawford McDonald
—*Courtesy of Crawford McDonald*

Joe Kelly (in his plane)

—*Courtesy of Tony Kelly*

Chapter XXXII
13 Messerschmitt 109 Pilots

Story of Joseph Kelly

COLONEL KELLY BEGAN HIS TRAINING IN JUNE 1938 when he graduated from Eastern Illinois University with a degree in Chemistry. As soon as he graduated he entered flight training at Randolph Field in San Antonio, TX. His class initially had about 100 cadets. Approximately 80% of the class washed out. Kelly graduated 2nd in his class in September 1938. He continued his officers' training at Randolph Field and was then commissioned to 2nd Lieutenant in May of 1939.

Joseph Kelly arrived in London in 1941, he was brought over by the Battleship Rodney. The German "blitz was full on". He was with 11 other American Fighter Pilots that were observers to the British courage from the ground and from the air. Happ Arnold was his superior.

Joseph's first lodging was a formidable church rectory out a little from London. He would stand in his doorway after the British 30 and 50 caliber machine guns "burped up" at the German bombers. He was warned that lead had to come back down and it could penetrate roofs very easily. He knew that door frames would give extra protection, so that is where he stood.

Joseph would fly as an observer near the British bombers, only to the French border and then he would return to England. He was attached to the 242 Fighter Squadron RAF Hurricanes in Wealed, England. They were all being trained for America's impending entry into WWII. During the summer of 1941, Hitler turned his wrath on Russia and invaded her.

The twelve observer American pilots in England during 1941 received an invitation by King George VI and Queen Mary to be honored. They were wined and dined at Windsor Castle. Joseph was introduced to King George and Queen Mary. He shook the King's cold hand too hard. George VI stuttered and the Queen was very open, friendly, and most gracious to all of them.

Joseph told me: "Fancy hotel penthouse rooms in London were at a very low rate. They were real bargains, because of the German daily bombings. According to the 11 American pilots and Joseph, the British people were very brave. They co-operated and supported the British government. They were part of a fierce resistance against Hitler's Nazi tyranny.

The War then progressed thru 1941 and 1942 with Joseph being transferred to North Africa and then on to Italy.

Joseph's job in Africa was to help coordinate the dive bomber's attacks and tank movements against Rommel's Africa core. He was stationed there around 2 years. While stationed in North Africa, Joseph met George Patton. He remembered a funny story involving General Patton that happened while he was there. Patton's troops had captured a German halftrack. As a joke, they placed it in front of Patton's headquarters with the machine gun still attached and pointing towards the door. When Patton woke up and looked out, he thought that the Germans had taken over the city during the night and he, along with some of his staff, fled the building, and hid in a nearby barn. When they were "discovered" they were standing in manure planning their escape. He was not very amused when he found that it was a prank.

The 522th Fighter Squadron, which Joseph was a member of, was later stationed 20 miles south of Salerno, Italy. He was flying the American A36 aircraft. On December 21, 1943, northwest of Rome, Joseph got separated from his fellow pilots in some clouds. He sighted a Heinkel III (a German military passenger plane) east of the Alban Hills. Heinkel's were used to ferry pilots in order to pick up new planes. They had previously been used as bombers in the invasion of France. Joseph had lucked up and got on its tail. It had 13 German fighter pilots inside in addition to the crew. He said he "shot it up coming and going". It lost altitude quickly and fell, striking a high tension electrical transmission line. Its left wing fell off and it burned as it hit the farmland below.

Joseph learned, in June of 1944, that 17 people were aboard the Heinkel III. He visited the wreckage, which was located in a farm's field. It had been used as a chicken loop by the local farmers. He found the map for the planes line of flight in the cockpit. Joseph also retrieved a piece of the thick bullet proof glass that was intended to protect the pilots from antiaircraft fire. He still has it, I have seen it. Its goal was to fly to Munich and then fly to Augsburg, Germany and pick up thirteen new Messerschmitt 109 planes. Joseph's big kill helped the Allies take Italy with fewer casualties.

When he was stationed in Italy, he read the book *The Principles of War* by Karl Von Clausewitz. The book was a reprint with certain sections italicized. Those were ones that the Germans believed to be the most important. Joseph used this book to further develop his aviation skills and to eliminate tactics and maneuvers that were unwarranted or avoidable.

Joseph's plane was a P51 Mustang- with dive brakes that the Army Air Force called the A36. It suited his temperament, calm, cool, and collected; he never got unglued or flew off the handle. He rarely lost his composure or his steadfastness.

Throughout WWII, Joseph was shot at by Germans and a British battle ship (near Salerno, Italy). He was also shot at by Allied troops in Italy and he occasionally returned their friendly fire. Friendly fire was a common occurrence in WWII. Joseph remembered up to 14 instances where bombs were dropped or they fired shots on fellow Allied troops in one day. War is hell and confusion.

Throughout WWII, Joseph was shot at by Germans and a British battle ship (near Salerno, Italy). He was also shot at by Allied troops in

Italy and he occasionally returned their friendly fire. Friendly fire was a common occurrence in WWII. Joseph remembered up to 14 instances where bombs were dropped or they fired shots on fellow Allied troops in one day. War is hell and confusion.

Joseph's remarkable service record includes 92 combat missions over England, North Africa, and Italy. He received the Distiguished Flying Cross and six other air medals, and seven battle stars. Joseph also served our country in Korea and worked with the CIA in Vietnam. He has flown the following planes: PT9- Primary Trainer9, P12 Fighter built by Boeing, A20 bomber Airline built by Grumman, BT9- Basic Trainer 9 built by Grumman, B10 bomber built by Grumman, P 38, P40, and P51 Mustang.

Joseph was written about in Peter C. Smith's book "Straight Down!" (See pages 156-163). It includes pictures of the Heinkel III and of his A36 plane called *Bee Ann*. The book also describes many other WWII air battles in which the A36 dive-bombers participated.

Joe Kelly with his granddaughter, Jill.

—*Courtesy of Tony Kelly*

SELECTED REFERENCES

The Rising Sun, World War II, Time Life Books
    By Arthur Zich, Alexandria, VA

A 50th Anniversary History, World War II, The Associated Press
    By Henry Holt and Company, New York

Battle of the Bulge, World War II, Time Life Books
    Chicago, IL

The Attack on Pearl Harbor, The Personal Journal of Captain Mike
    Burbage
    Captain Mike Burbage

Until The Final Gun, First Books Library
    Norma Rogers

Band of Brothers, Simon & Schuster
    Stephen E. Ambrose

Pacific War 1941 - 1945, Quill 1982, NYNY
    John Costello

Sky Giants Over Japan, Apollo Books, Winona, MN
    By Chester Marshall

Global Twentieth Century
    By Chester Marshall

Seahorse Soldiering, Libris Corp.
    By Robert Meredith Watson, Jr.

Straight Down, Crecy Publishing, 2000, Manchester, M22 5LH
    By Peter C. Smith

Reuinion in Tokyko
    Journal by Sam Weintraub

The Parade
    Journal by Simon "Spider Webb"

The United States Army 106 Infantry Division- Battle of the Bulge
    Journal by Walter J. Phelan Jr.

The Ranch
    Journal by Simon "Spider" Webb

The Navigator
    Journal by Hank Brukardt

The Second World War, Their Finest Hour, by Winston S. Churchill,
    Houghton Mifflin Company- Boston, The Riverside Press-
    Cambridge, 1949

The Concise Guide to American Aircraft of World War II, David
    Mondey, 1996, Smithmark Publishers

Lightning: The History of the 78th Infantry Division, edited by The Division
    Historical Association, The Battery Press—Nashville, 2000
    The Tuskegee Airmen
    www.acepilots.com

National Geographic, 17th and M Sts. N.W., Washington, D.C., 20036.
    May 1995
    National Archives
    www.nationalarchives.com

The B24 Pilot and the End of the Japanese Empire
    Journal by Crawford McDonald

ABOUT THE AUTHOR
Victor and Kay Robilio

Victor L. Robilio Jr., graduated from the University of Memphis in 1962 with a BBA. *The Way It Was* is Victor's fourth book. Victor resides in Memphis, Tennessee and has a weekend home in Oxford, Mississippi, very close to the University of Mississippi campus. Victor is a history buff, wine expert, and business owner.

The Way It Was is a collection of journals and oral interviews that he has collected and done himself. Victor has interviewed over 200 war heroes. Victor has written this book from his heart and he hopes that you value it as much as he does!

The PBS WKNO-TV preview for the documentary THE WAR—a Ken Burns film, held in Memphis, Tenn. (Left to Right: Ken Burns, Victor L. Robilio Jr., and Charles Lambert)

—*Courtesy of The Best Times, Lester Gingold (photographer)*